CW00665967

HAR...

BISHOP'S STORTFORD

www.philips-maps.co.uk

First published 2008 by

Philip's, a division of
Octopus Publishing Group Ltd
www.octopusbooks.co.uk
2–4 Heron Quays
London E14 4JP
An Hachette Livre UK Company
www.hachettelivre.co.uk

First edition 2008
First impression 2008

ISBN 978-0-540-09371-7

© Philip's 2008

This product includes mapping data licensed
from Ordnance Survey®, with the permission
of the Controller of Her Majesty's Stationery
Office.

© Crown copyright 2008. All rights reserved.
Licence number 100011710

Printed and bound in China by Toppan

Contents

II Key to map symbols

III Key to map pages

IV Route planning

2 Street maps at 4½ inches to 1 mile

46 Index

58 List of numbered locations

Key to map symbols

Roads

Motorway with junction number

Primary route – dual, single carriageway

A road – dual, single carriageway

B road – dual, single carriageway

Through-route – dual, single carriageway

Minor road – dual, single carriageway

Rural track, private road or narrow road in urban area

Path, bridleway, byway open to all traffic, road used as a public path

Road under construction

Pedestrianised area

Gate or obstruction to traffic restrictions may not apply at all times or to all vehicles

Parking, Park and Ride

Speed cameras – single, multiple

Railways

Railway

Miniature railway

Metro station, private railway station

Emergency services

Ambulance station, coastguard station

Fire station, police station

Hospital, Accident and Emergency entrance to hospital

General features

Place of worship, Post Office

Information centre (open all year)

Bus or coach station, shopping centre

Important buildings, schools, colleges, universities and hospitals

Woods, built-up area

Tumulus FORT **Non-Roman antiquity, Roman antiquity**

Leisure facilities

 Camping site, caravan site

Golf course, picnic site

Boundaries

• • • • • • • • **Postcode boundaries**

County and unitary authority boundaries

Water features

River
Ouse **Tidal water, water name**

Non-tidal water – lake, river, canal or stream

< | **Lock, weir**

Scales

Blue pages: 4½ inches to 1 mile   1:14 080

| 0 | 220 yds | ¼ mile | 660 yds | ½ mile |

| 0 | 125m | 250m | 375m | ½ km |

44 **Adjoining page indicators** The mapping continues on the page indicated by the arrow

Abbreviations

Acad	Academy		Mkt	Market
Allot Gdns	Allotments		Meml	Memorial
Cemy	Cemetery		Mon	Monument
C Ctr	Civic Centre		Mus	Museum
CH	Club House		Obsy	Observatory
Coll	College		Pal	Royal Palace
Crem	Crematorium		PH	Public House
Ent	Enterprise		Recn Gd	Recreation Ground
Ex H	Exhibition Hall		Resr	Reservoir
Ind Est	Industrial Estate		Ret Pk	Retail Park
IRB Sta	Inshore Rescue Boat Station		Sch	School
			Sh Ctr	Shopping Centre
Inst	Institute		TH	Town Hall/House
Ct	Law Court		Trad Est	Trading Estate
L Ctr	Leisure Centre		Univ	University
LC	Level Crossing		Wks	Works
Liby	Library		YH	Youth Hostel

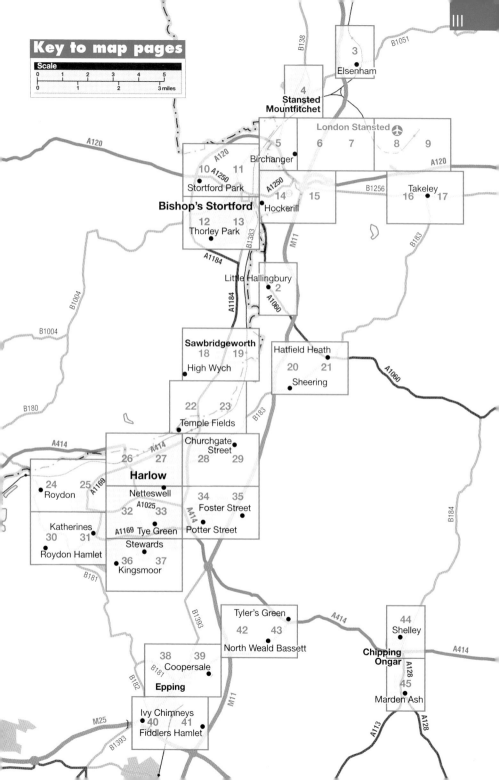

Key to map pages

Scale

0 1 2 3 4 5

0 1 2 3 miles

B138

B1051

3

Elsenham

4

Stansted Mountfitchet

A120

London Stansted ✈

5 6 7 8 9

A1250 Birchanger A120

10 11

A120 A1250

Stortford Park

A1250 14 15 B1256 Takeley

Hockerill 16 17

Bishop's Stortford

12 13

Thorley Park B1383

A1184

B183

A1184

Little Hallingbury

A1060 2

B1004 M11

B1004

Sawbridgeworth

18 19

High Wych Hatfield Heath

20 21

Sheering

A1060

22 23

Temple Fields B183

B180

Churchgate Street

A414 28 29

A414

26 27

Harlow

24 25 Netteswell 34 35 Foster Street

Roydon A1169 A1025

32 33 A414

A1169 Tye Green Potter Street

Katherines Stewards

30 31

Roydon Hamlet 36 37

Kingsmoor

B181 B184

B1393 Tyler's Green

42 43

North Weald Bassett

A414 44 Shelley

38 39 **Chipping Ongar** A414

B181 Coopersale A128

B182 **Epping** 45

M11 Marden Ash

M25 Ivy Chimneys A113 A128

40 41

B1393 Fiddlers Hamlet

III

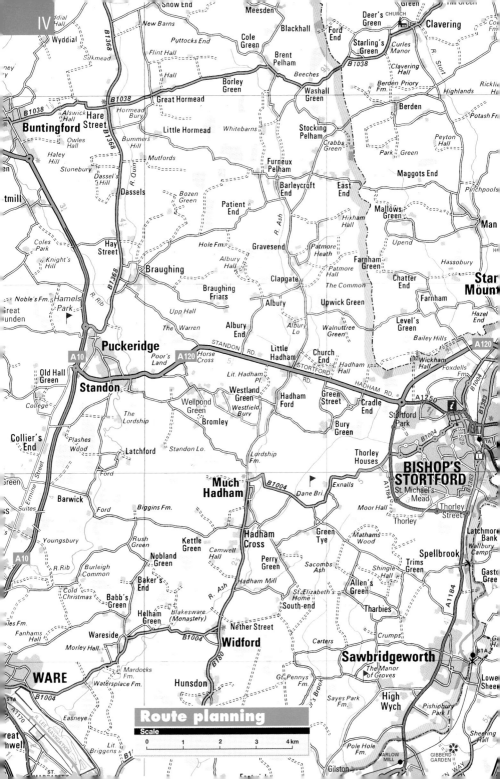

Route planning

Scale

0   1   2   3   4 km

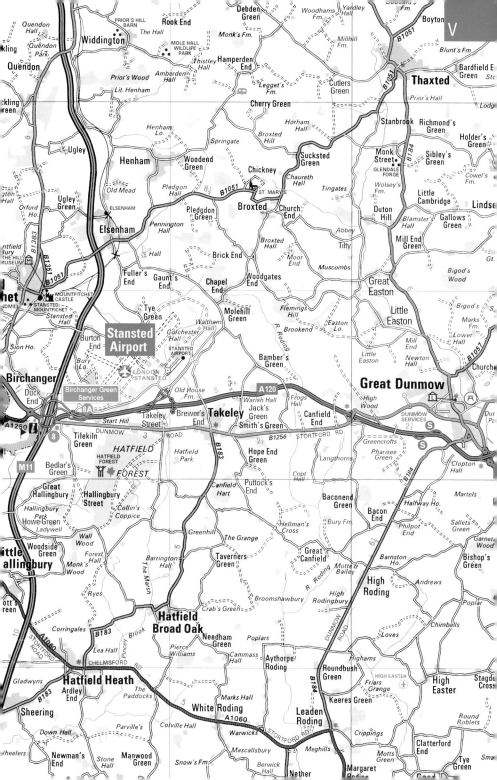

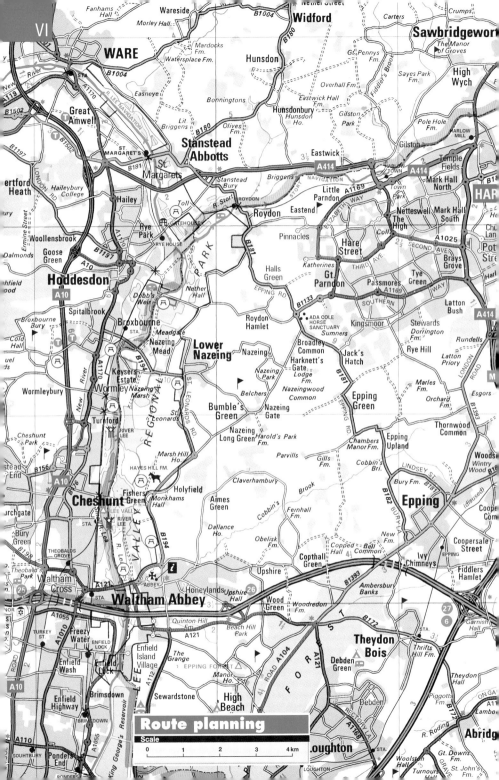

Route planning

Scale

| 0 | 1 | 2 | 3 | 4 km |

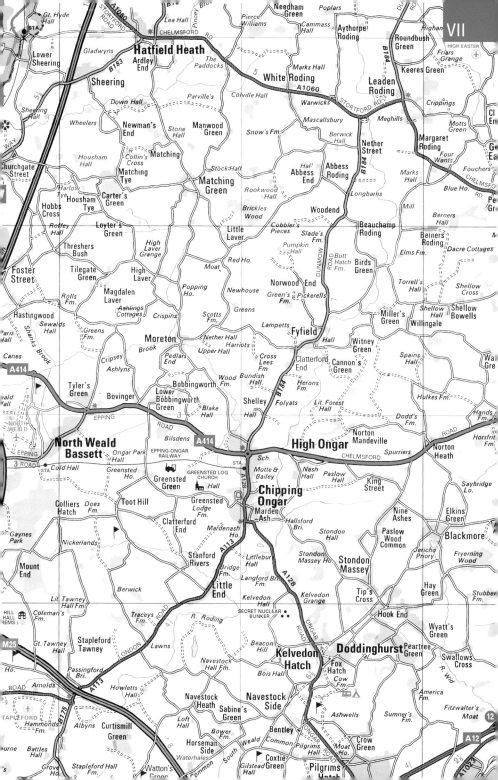

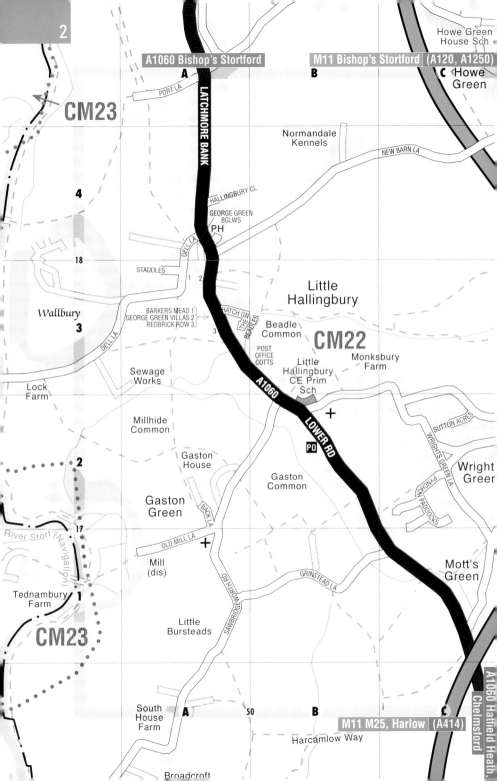

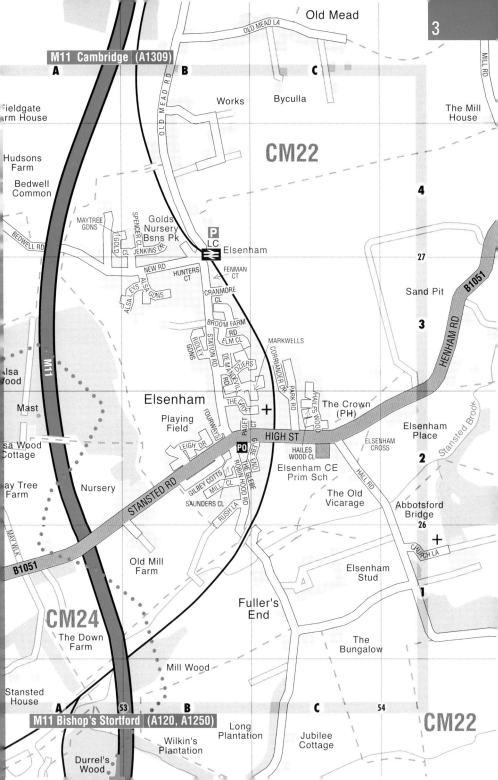

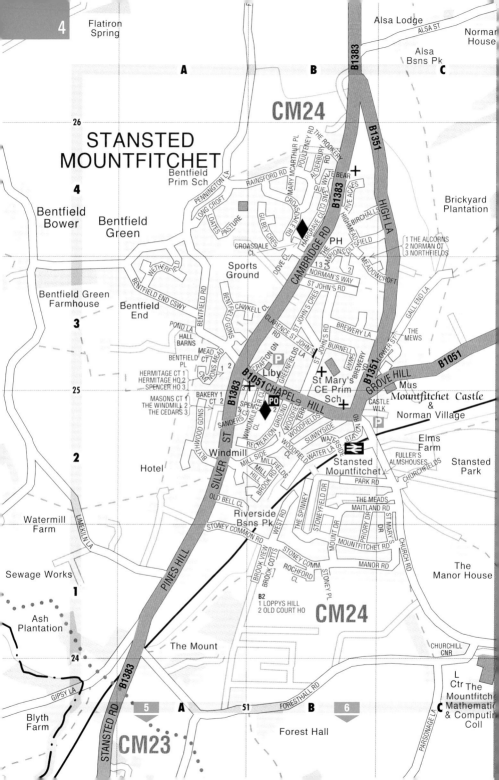

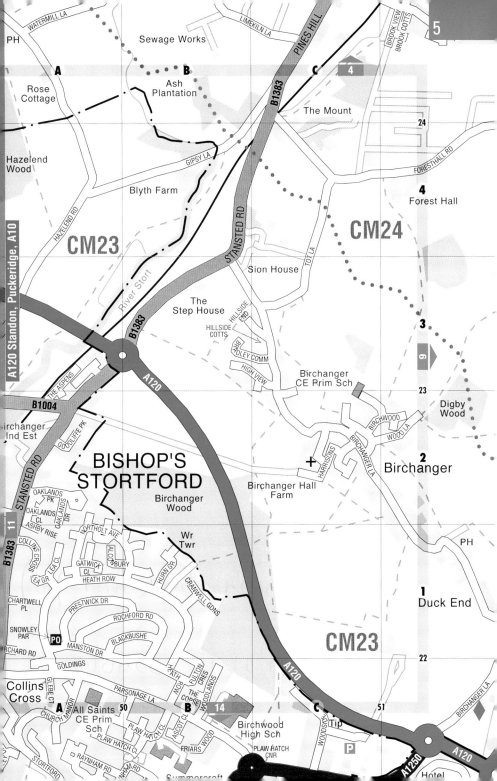

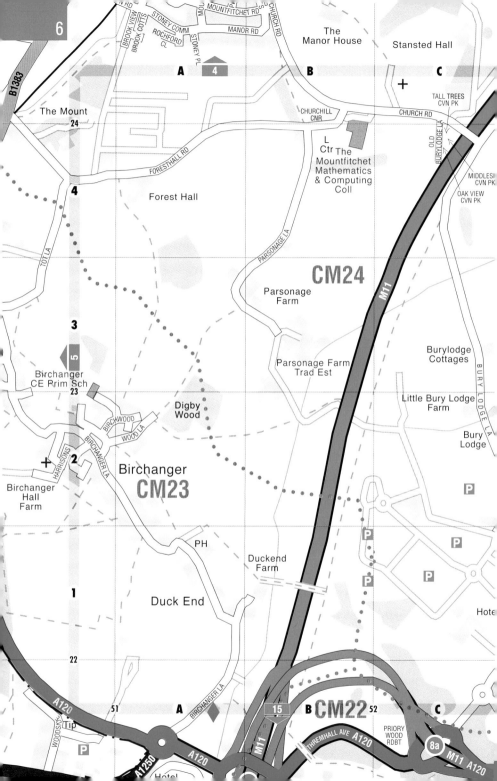

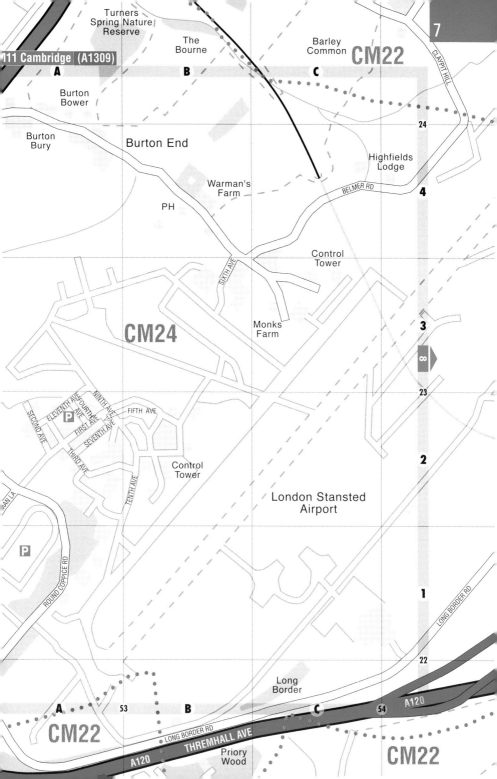

Turners
Spring Nature
Reserve

The
Bourne

Barley
Common
CM22

M11 Cambridge (A1309)

A
B
C

CLAYPIT HILL

Burton
Bower

24

Burton
Bury

Burton End

Highfields
Lodge

Warman's
Farm

BELMER RD

4

PH

Control
Tower

SIXTH AVE

CM24

Monks
Farm

3

8

23

NINTH AVE
ELEVENTH AVE
FOURTH AVE
FIFTH AVE
FIRST AVE
SECOND AVE
SEVENTH AVE
THIRD AVE
TENTH AVE

P

Control
Tower

2

London Stansted
Airport

P

ROUND COPPICE RD

LONG BORDER RD

1

22

Long
Border

A
53
B
C
54
A120

CM22

LONG BORDER RD
THREMHALL AVE
A120

Priory
Wood

CM22

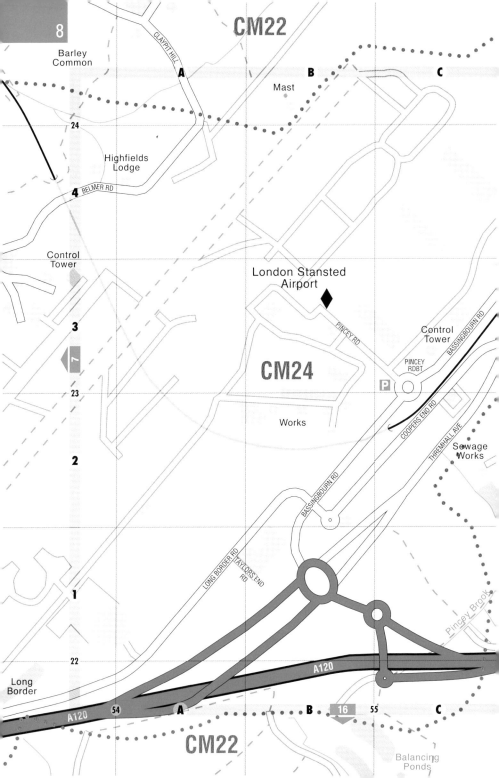

CM22

Barley
Common

A   B   C

CLAYPIT HILL

Mast

24

Highfields
Lodge

4 BELMER RD

Control
Tower

London Stansted
Airport

PINCEY RD

Control
Tower

BASSINGBOURN RD

3

PINCEY
RDBT

7

P

COOPERS END RD

23

CM24

THREMHALL AVE

Works

Sewage
Works

2

BASSINGBOURN RD

1

LONG BORDER RD

TAYLORS END
RD

Pincey Brook

22

A120

Long
Border

A120   54   A   B   16   55   C

CM22

Balancing
Ponds

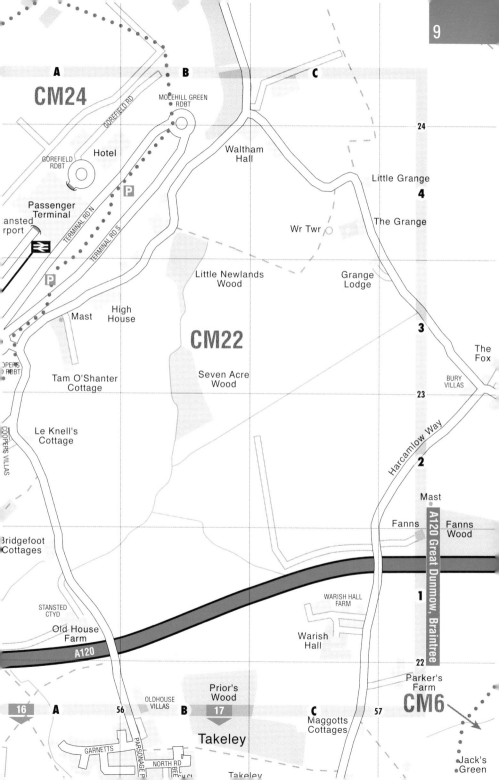

A   B   C

CM24

GOREFIELD RD

MOLEHILL GREEN
RDBT

24

Hotel

Waltham
Hall

Little Grange

4

GOREFIELD
RDBT

P

Passenger
Terminal

The Grange

ansted
rport

Wr Twr

Little Newlands
Wood

Grange
Lodge

P

TERMINAL RD N

TERMINAL RD S

Mast

High
House

CM22

3

The
Fox

OPERS
RDBT

Tam O'Shanter
Cottage

Seven Acre
Wood

BURY
VILLAS

23

Le Knell's
Cottage

COOPERS
VILLAS

Harcamlow Way

2

Mast

Fanns

A120 Great Dunmow, Braintree

Fanns
Wood

Bridgefoot
Cottages

1

STANSTED
CTYD

WARISH HALL
FARM

Old House
Farm

A120

Warish
Hall

22

Parker's
Farm

16   A   56

OLDHOUSE
VILLAS

Prior's
Wood

B   17

C   57

CM6

Maggotts
Cottages

GARNETTS

PARSONAGE

NORTH RD

Takeley

Takeley

Jack's
Green

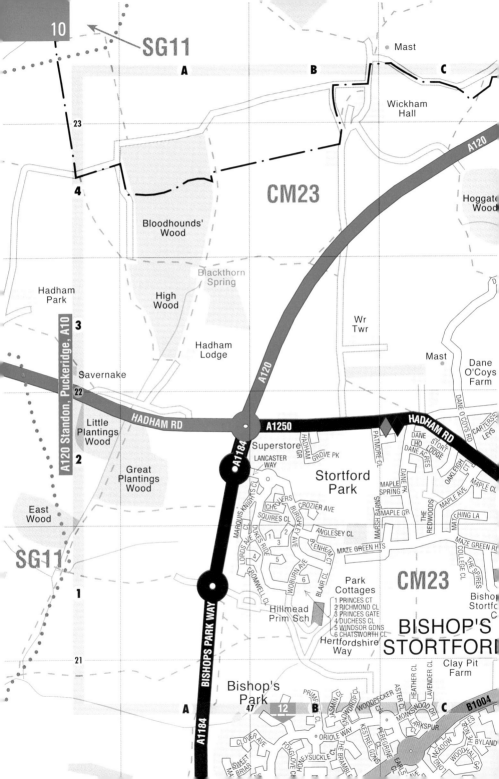

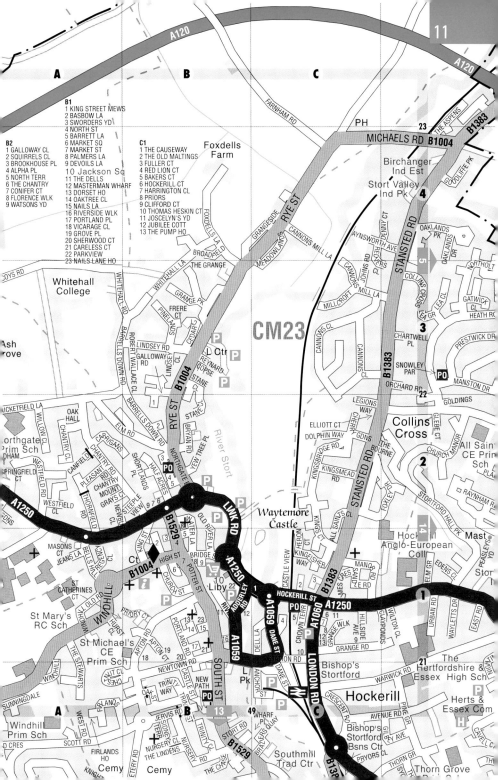

B1
1 KING STREET MEWS
2 BASBOW LA
3 SWORDERS YD
4 NORTH ST
5 BARRETT LA
6 MARKET SQ
7 MARKET ST
8 PALMERS LA
9 DEVOILS LA
10 JACKSON SQ
11 THE DELLS
12 MASTERMAN WHARF
13 DORSET HO
14 OAKTREE CL
15 NAILS LA
16 RIVERSIDE WLK
17 PORTLAND PL
18 VICARAGE CL
19 GROVE PL
20 SHERWOOD CT
21 CARELESS CT
22 PARKVIEW
23 NAILS LANE HO

B2
1 GALLOWAY CL
2 SQUIRRELS CL
3 BROOKHOUSE PL
4 ALPHA PL
5 NORTH TERR
6 THE CHANTRY
7 CONIFER CT
8 FLORENCE WLK
9 WATSONS YD

C1
1 THE CAUSEWAY
2 THE OLD MALTINGS
3 FULLER CT
4 RED LION CT
5 BAKERS CT
6 HOCKERILL CT
7 HARRINGTON CL
8 PRIORS
9 CLIFFORD CT
10 THOMAS HESKIN CT
11 JOSCELYN'S YD
12 JUBILEE COTT
13 THE PUMP HO

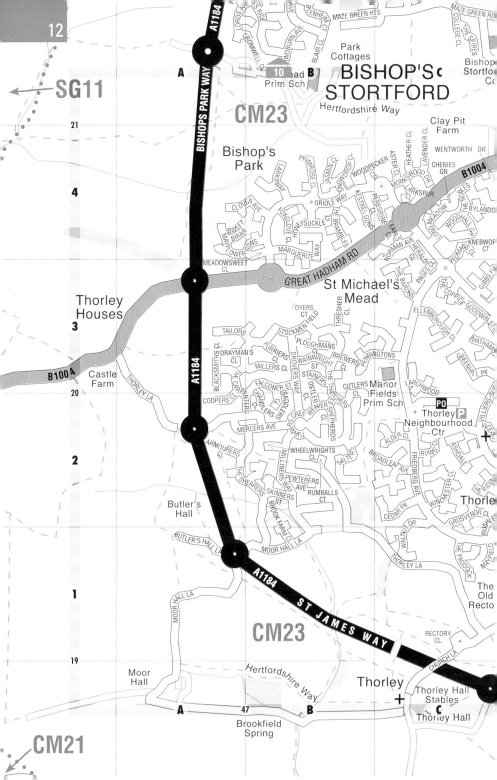

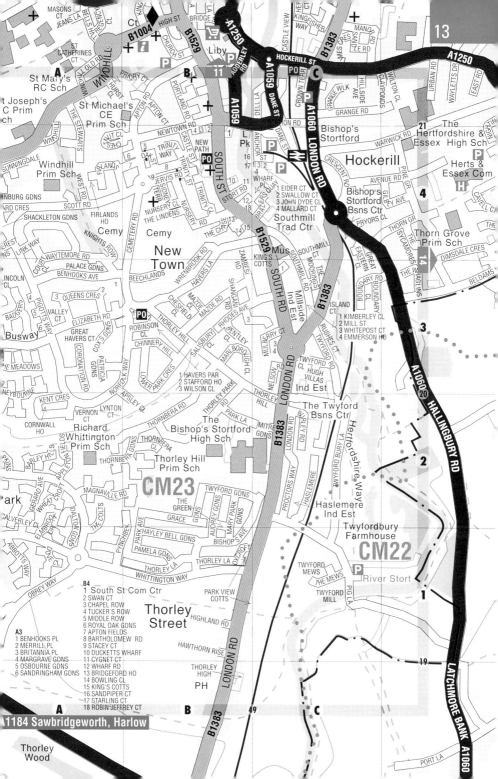

MASONS CT
JEANS LA
BELLS HILL
KING ST
HIGH ST
B1004
St CATHERINES CT
Liby
i
CHURCH ST
B1529
BRIDGE ST
LA
A1250
AUDLEY RD
CASTLE VIEW
HELENS
KINGFISHER WAY
CRES
MANOR RD
SANDZERD
B1383
HOCKERILL ST
A1250
WILTON RD
URBAN RD
EAST RD
WAYLETTS RD

A
St Mary's RC Sch
WINDHILL
PRIORY CT
HURST LA
OLD RD
11
P
11
A1059
A1059
DANE ST
B
A1059
CROWN TERR
A1060
PO
C
GRANGE WLK
HILLSIDE AVE
CLAYPONDS
GRANGE RD
21
The Hertfordshire & Essex High Sch

t Joseph's C Prim ch
St Michael's CE Prim Sch
THE STEWARTS
NUT CL
APTON CT
APTON RD
NEWTOWN RD
NEW PATH
TRINITY WAY
TRIN
8
STATION RD
A1060
LONDON RD
Bishop's Stortford
WARWICK RD
Hockerill
AVENUE RD
PINE AVE
Herts & Essex Com
H
CAVELL RD

SUNNINGDALE
Windhill Prim Sch
WEST RD
FLANDS
L Pk
NEW PATH
P0
2
JERVIS RD
JESMINE CL
TRINITY RD
NURSERY CL
9
16
17
15
WHARF PL
1
BRAZIERS QUAY
1 EIDER CT
2 SWALLOW CT
3 JOHN DYDE CL
4 MALLARD CT
Bishop's Stortford Bsns Ctr
PRYORS CL
GREAT EASTERN CL
4
Thorn Grove Prim Sch
DIMSDALE CRES
THE SYCAMORES
BELDAMS

NBURG GDNS
RD CRES
SHACKLETON GDNS
FIRLANDS HO
KNIGHTS ROW
Cemy
Cemy
New Town
WRENBROOK RD
HAVERS LA
MAZOE RD
SHANGANI RD
KING'S COTTS
Southmill Trad Ctr
Mus
SOUTHMILL RD
Millside Ind Est
B1529
SOUTH RD
B1383
14
THE WAGLINS

CREST
LINK WAY
NS
INCOLN CL
QUEENS CRES
BENHOOKS AVE
PALACE GDNS
3
VALLEY CT
ELIZABETH RD
GREAT HAVERS CT
Busway
CHINNERY HILL
THORLEY HILL
ROBINSON CL
CHESFIELD CL
MAJOR RD
RHODES AVE
BRENTLEY
SALISBURY RD
MULBERRY CT
3
4
Island
1 KIMBERLEY CL
2 MILL ST
3 WHITEPOST CT
4 EMMERSON HO
A1060
3

HE MEADOWS
NEYBOURNE
KENT CRES
VERNON CT
LYNTON CT
PATRICIA GDNS
CORONATION RD
NORFOLK WAY
APSLEY CT
LOWER PARK CRES
1 HAVERS PAR
2 STAFFORD HO
3 WILSON CL
MARLBOROUGH CL
NELSON RD
LONDON RD
TWYFORD CL
HUGH VILLAS
TWYFORD RD
Ind Est
The Twyford Bsns Ctr
HALLINGBURY RD
20
2

CORNWALL HO
Richard Whittington Prim Sch
THORNBERA GDNS
THORNBERA RD
THORNBERA GDNS
PARK LA
THE Bishop's Stortford High Sch
MITRE GDNS
B1383
BARLEY RD
PROCTORS WAY
HASLEMERE
TWYFORD BURY LA
Hertfordshire Way

BARLEY HLS
FIELDS
GERARD AVE
MAGNAVILLE RD
Thorley Hill Prim Sch
THORNBERA RD
THE GREEN
GRACE GDNS
AUDREY GDNS
MARY PARK GDNS
BISHOP'S AVE
Haslemere Ind Est
Twyfordbury Farmhouse
CM22
1

ark
WHEAT CROFT
APPLETON FIELDS
ELMBROOK GDNS
DALTON GDNS
THE COLTS
CM23
PYNCHBEK
PARK AVE
HAYLEY BELL GDNS
PAMELA GDNS
TWYFORD GDNS
HAYLEY RD
TWYFORD MEWS
THE MEWS
P
River Stort
PIG LA
2

CALVERLEY CL
ABBOTS WAY
OBREY WAY
THORLEY LA
WHITTINGTON WAY
THORLEY LA
PARK VIEW COTTS
HIGHLAND RD
Thorley Street
LONDON RD
B1383
HAWTHORN RISE
TWYFORD MILL
19

B4
1 South St Com Ctr
2 SWAN CT
3 CHAPEL ROW
4 TUCKER S ROW
5 MIDDLE ROW
6 ROYAL OAK GDNS
7 APTON FIELDS
8 BARTHOLOMEW RD
9 STACEY CT
10 DUCKETTS WHARF
11 CYGNET CT
12 WHARF RD
13 BRIDGEFORD HO
14 BOWLING CL
15 KING'S COTTS
16 SANDPIPER CT
17 STARLING CT
18 ROBIN JEFFREY CT

A3
1 BENHOOKS PL
2 MERRILL PL
3 BRITANNIA PL
4 MARGRAVE GDNS
5 OSBOURNE GDNS
6 SANDRINGHAM GDNS

THORLEY HIGH PH

A
B
49
C

Thorley Wood

LATCHMORE BANK
A1060
PORT LA

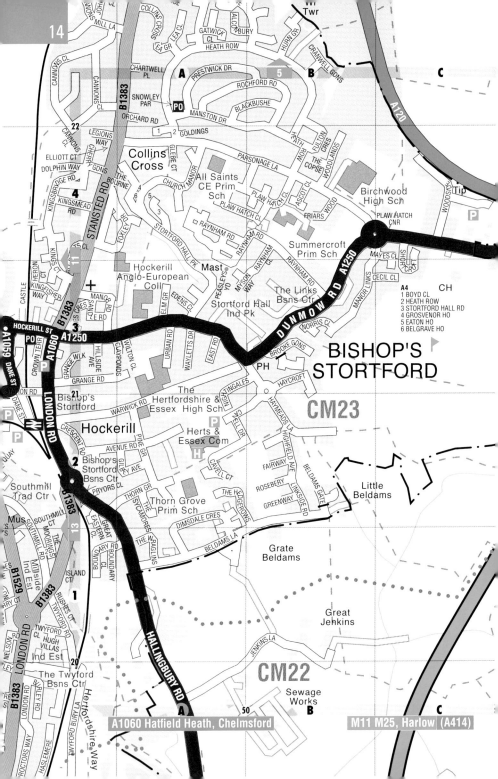

COLLINS CROSS
GATWICK CL
ALCONBURY
HURN GR
Wr Twr
HEATH ROW
CRANWELL GDNS
CHARTWELL PL
A
PRESTWICK DR
B
5
C
SNOWLEY PAR
PO
ROCHFORD RD
B1383
MANSTON DR
BLACKBUSHE
A120
CANNONS CL
ORCHARD RD
1
2
GOLDINGS
22
CANNONS CL
LEGIONS WAY
CHERRY
PARSONAGE LA
ELLIOTT CT
GDNS
Collins
DOLPHIN WAY
THE BOURNE
Cross
GLEBE CT
CHURCH MANOR
All Saints
CE Prim
Sch
FULTON CRES
HEATH
THE COPSE
WOODLANDS
Birchwood
High Sch
Tip
KINGSBRIDGE RD
4
KINGSMEAD RD
4
5
3
PLAW HATCH CL
ASCOT CL
FRIARS
WOOD
P
STANSTED RD
RAYNHAM RD
STORTFORD HALL PK
PLAW HATCH CL
PLAW HATCH CNR
FOXLEYD
RAYNHAM RD
Summercroft
Prim Sch
MAYES CL
KINGS CL
HERON CT
11
Hockerill
Anglo-European
Coll
MANOR RD
EDENS CL
PEASLEYS YD
Mast
MYSON
RAYNHAM CL
RAYNHAM RD
The Links
Bsns Ctr
A1250
DUNMOW RD
SHORT CR
CECIL CL
MANOR LINKS
A4
1 BOYD CL
2 HEATH ROW
3 STORTFORD HALL RD
4 GROSVENOR HO
5 EATON HO
6 BELGRAVE HO
CH
CASTLE
KINGFISHER WAY
B1383
SANDLE RD
ELM GR
Stortford Hall
Ind Pk
NORRIS CL
BISHOP'S
STORTFORD
HOCKERILL ST
A1250
HILLSIDE AVE
URBAN RD
EAST RD
WAYLETTS DR
WILTON CL
CLAYPONDS
BROOKE GDNS
PH
HAYCROFT
A1069
PO
CROWN TERR
GRANGE WLK
GRANGE RD
A1060
Bishop's
Stortford
21
WARWICK RD
The
Hertfordshire &
Essex High Sch
TINGALES
HAYMEADS LA
CM23
STATION RD
DANE ST
P
LONDON RD
Hockerill
AVENUE RD
PINE GR
Herts &
Essex Com
H
CHELLOR
FAIRWAY
DANE ST
P
CRESCENT RD
GILBY AVE
2
Bishop's
Stortford
Bsns Ctr
CAVELL CT
ROSEBERY
HIGHFIELD AVE
LINKSIDE RD
BELDAMS GATE
Little
Beldams
PBYORS CL
THORN GR
GREENWAY
Southmill
Trad Ctr
THE SYCAMORES
Thorn Grove
Prim Sch
THE HEDGEROWS
Mus
B1383
SOUTHMILL CT
THE MOORINGS
DIMSDALE CRES
GREAT EASTERN CL
SOUTHMILL RD
Millside
Ind Est
MARY BOUNDARY
THE WRAGLINS
BELDAMS LA
Grate
Beldams
B1529
B1383
ISLAND CT
1
Great
Jenkins
NELSON CL
HUGH VILLAS
Ind Est
TWYFORD CL
RUSHES CT
TWYFORD RD
20
HALLINGBURY RD
JENKINS LA
LONDON RD
The Twyford
Bsns Ctr
CM22
B1383
PROCTORS WAY
Hertfordshire Way
HASLEMERE
TWYFORD BURY LA
A
50
Sewage
Works
B
C
A1060 Hatfield Heath, Chelmsford
M11 M25, Harlow (A414)

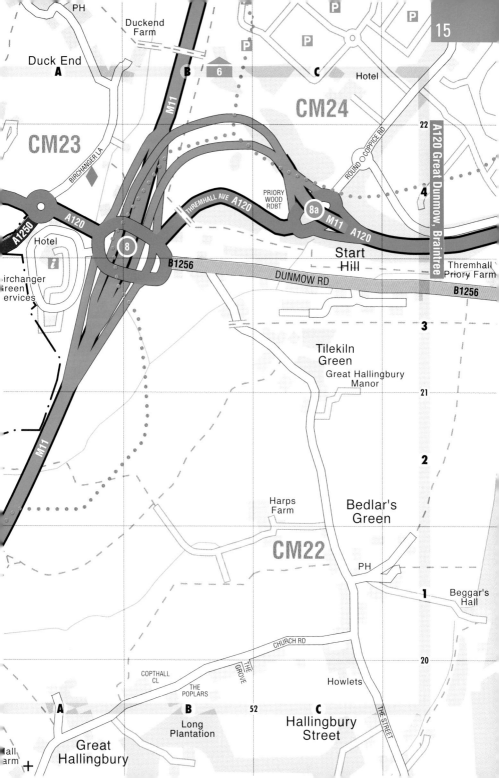

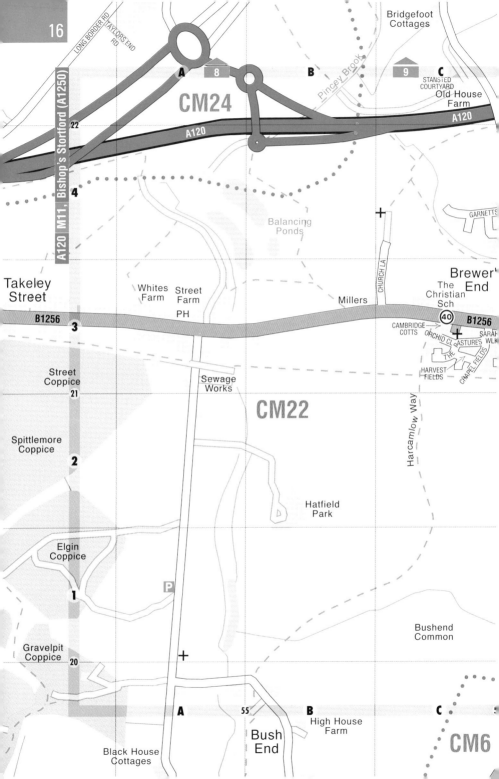

LONG BORDER RD
TAYLORS END RD

A

8

CM24

B

Pincey Brook

9

C

STANSTED COURTYARD
Old House Farm
Bridgefoot Cottages

A120

A1250

A120 M11, Bishop's Stortford (A1250)

22

4

GARNETTS

Balancing Ponds

CHURCH LA

Brewer' End
The Christian Sch

Takeley Street

Whites Farm

Street Farm PH

Millers

B1256

3

CAMBRIDGE COTTS

40

B1256

SARAH WLK

ORCHID CL PASTURES

THE

CHAPEL FIELDS

HARVEST FIELDS

Street Coppice

21

Sewage Works

CM22

Spittlemore Coppice

2

Harcamlow Way

Hatfield Park

Elgin Coppice

P

1

Bushend Common

Gravelpit Coppice

20

A

55

B

High House Farm

C

Black House Cottages

Bush End

CM6

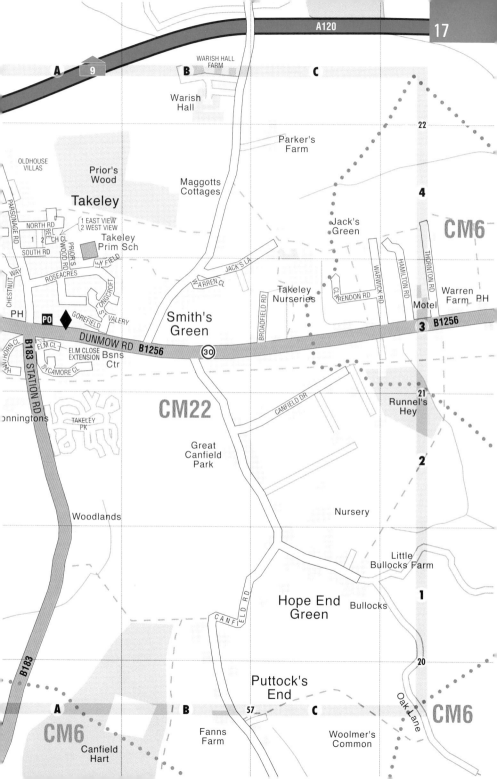

WARISH HALL FARM

Warish Hall

Parker's Farm

Maggotts Cottages

OLDHOUSE VILLAS

Prior's Wood

Takeley

1 EAST VIEW
2 WEST VIEW

PARSONAGE RD

NORTH RD

CH CL

1   2

SOUTH RD

Takeley Prim Sch

Jack's Green

WAY

PRIOR'S WOOD RD

ROSEACRES

LY FIELD

LONGCROFT

VALERY

CHESTNUT

WARREN CL

JACK'S LA

BROADFIELD RD

Takeley Nurseries

WARWICK RD

HAMILTON RD

CLARENDON RD

THORNTON RD

Warren Farm   PH

Motel

Smith's Green

GOREFIELD

PO

PH

DUNMOW RD   B1256

30

3   B1256

ELM CL

ELM CLOSE EXTENSION

SYCAMORE CL

HORN CL

B183 STATION RD

Bsns Ctr

onningtons

TAKELEY PK

CM22

Great Canfield Park

CANFIELD DR

Runnel's Hey

21

2

Woodlands

Nursery

Little Bullocks Farm

1

CANFIELD RD

Hope End Green

Bullocks

20

Puttock's End

Oak Lane

CM6

Canfield Hart

Fanns Farm

Woolmer's Common

B183

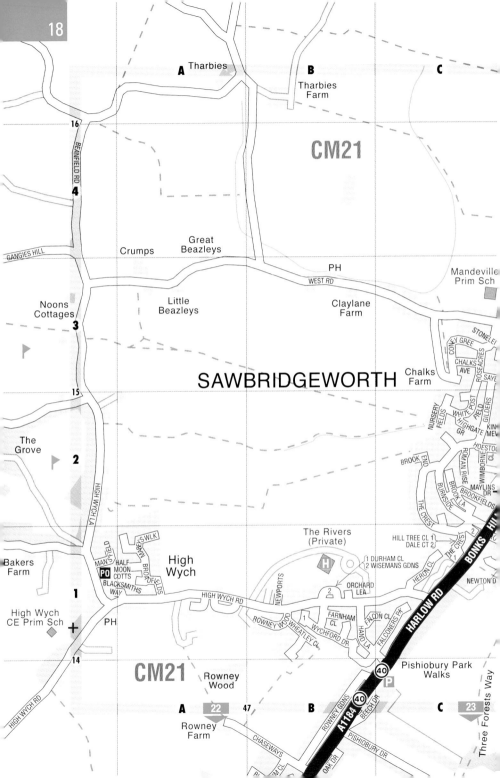

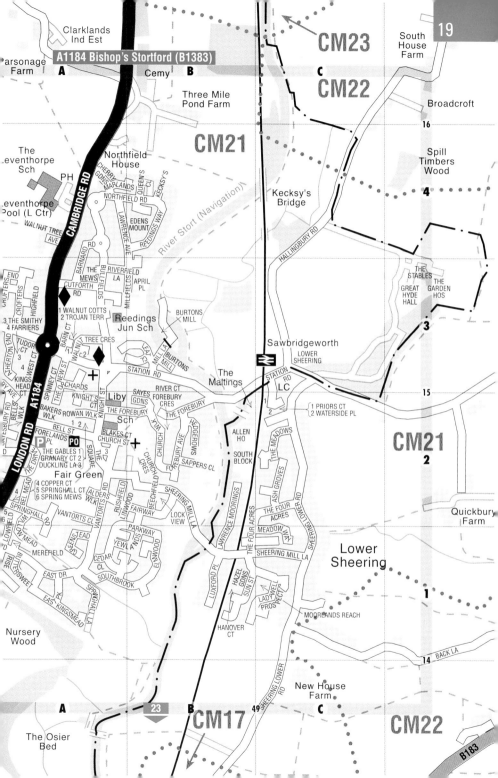

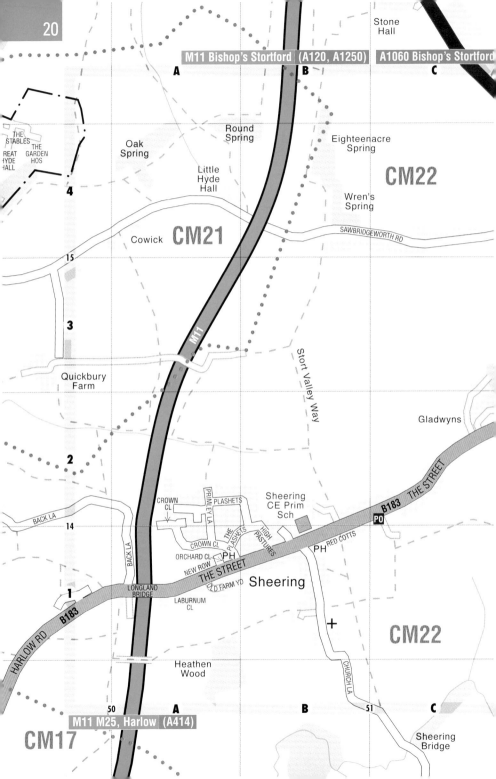

Stone
Hall

M11 Bishop's Stortford (A120, A1250) A1060 Bishop's Stortford

A   B   C

THE
STABLES
REAT   THE
HYDE   GARDEN
HALL   HOS

Oak
Spring

Round
Spring

Eighteenacre
Spring

CM22

Little
Hyde
Hall

Wren's
Spring

4

Cowick   CM21

SAWBRIDGEWORTH RD

15

3

M11

Quickbury
Farm

Stort Valley Way

Gladwyns

2

THE STREET

B183

CROWN
CL

PRIMLEY LA

PLASHETS

Sheering
CE Prim
Sch

PO

BACK LA

14

THE
PLASHETS

HIGH
PASTURES

RED COTTS

CROWN CL

BACK LA

ORCHARD CL   PH

NEW ROW

PH

THE STREET

Sheering

LONGLAND
BRIDGE

OLD FARM YD

1

B183

LABURNUM
CL

CHURCH LA

CM22

HARLOW RD

Heathen
Wood

50   A   B   51   C

M11 M25, Harlow (A414)

CM17

Sheering
Bridge

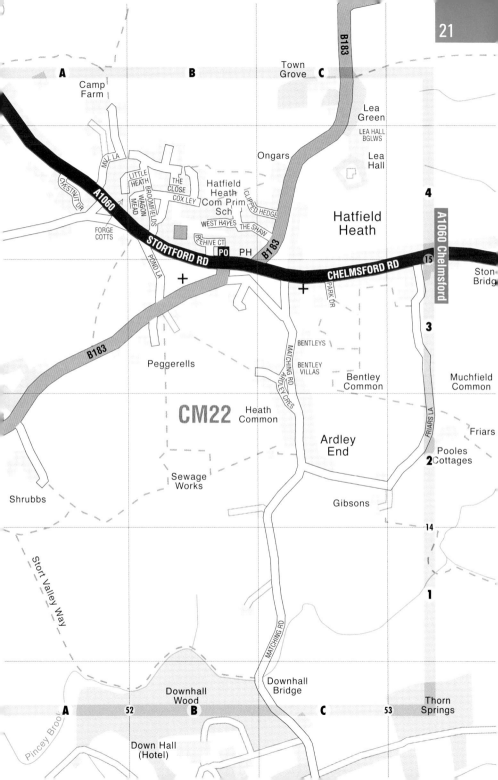

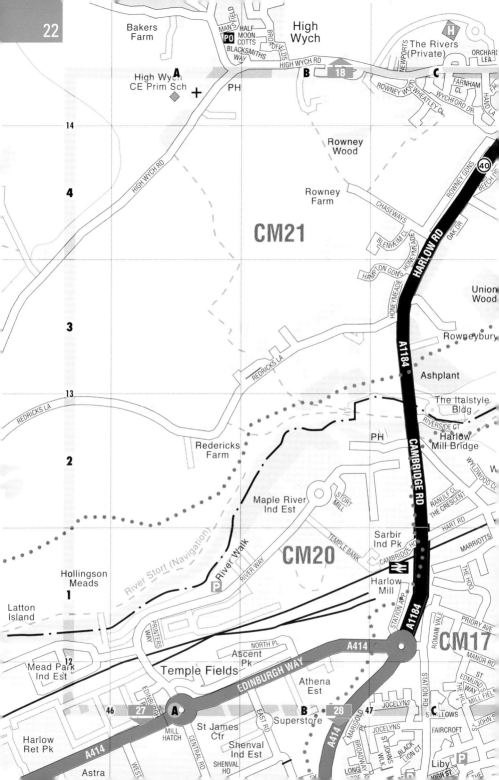

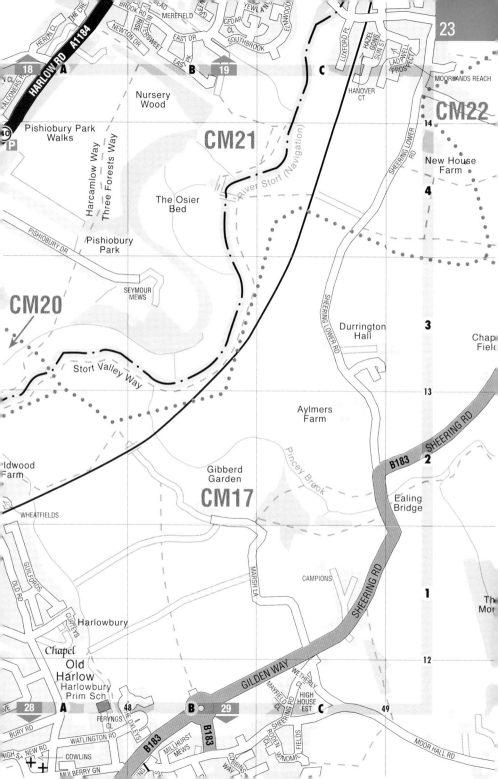

CM22

CM21

CM20

CM17

THE CRE
BROOK RD
MEREFIELD
HERON CL
NEWTON DR
BUTTERSWEET
EAST DR
EAST PK
SOUTHBROOK
CEDAR CL
YEWLAN
ELNWOOD

HARLOW RD A1184
FALCONERS

18 A

19 B

Nursery
Wood

Pishiobury Park
Walks

Harcamlow Way
Three Forests Way

PISHIOBURY DR

The Osier
Bed

Pishiobury
Park

SEYMOUR
MEWS

River Stort (Navigation)

Stort Valley Way

ldwood
Farm

WHEATFIELDS

GUILFORDS
OLD RD

CURTEYS

Harlowbury

Chapel
Old
Harlow

Harlowbury
Prim Sch

28 A

48

BURY RD

HIGH ST
NEW RD

FERYNGS
CL

OAKLEYS

COWLINS

MULBERRY GN

WATLINGTON RD

B183

MILLHURST
MEWS

Gibberd
Garden

MARSH LA

GILDEN WAY

B 29 B

B183

C

COBBINS
WAY

WNDMAI
RODEN CL
SHEERING RD
FIELDS

MAYFIELD
CL
WETHERLY
CL

HIGH
HOUSE
EST

CAMPIONS

Pincey Brook

Aylmers
Farm

Durrington
Hall

SHEERING LOWER RD

SHEERING LOWER RD

LUXFORD PL
HAZEL GDNS
SUN ST
LADYWELL
PROSPECT
HANOVER
CT

MOORLANDS REACH

New House
Farm

14

4

3

13

SHEERING RD

B183 2

Ealing
Bridge

SHEERING RD

Chap
Fiel

1

Th
Mor

12

49

MOOR HALL RD

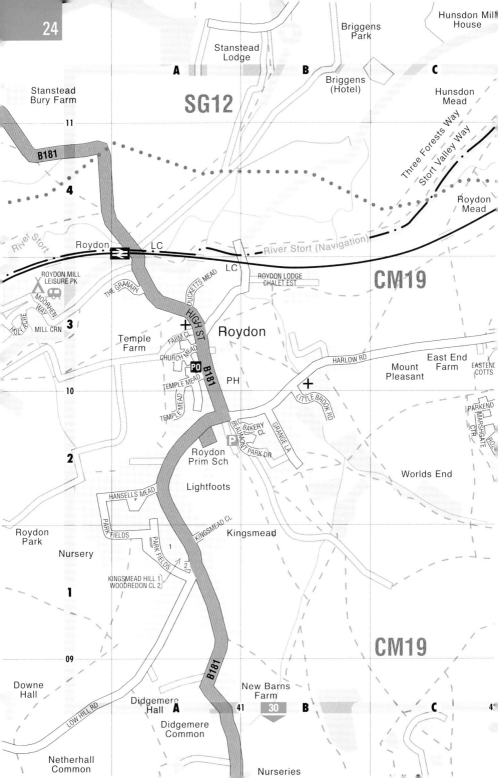

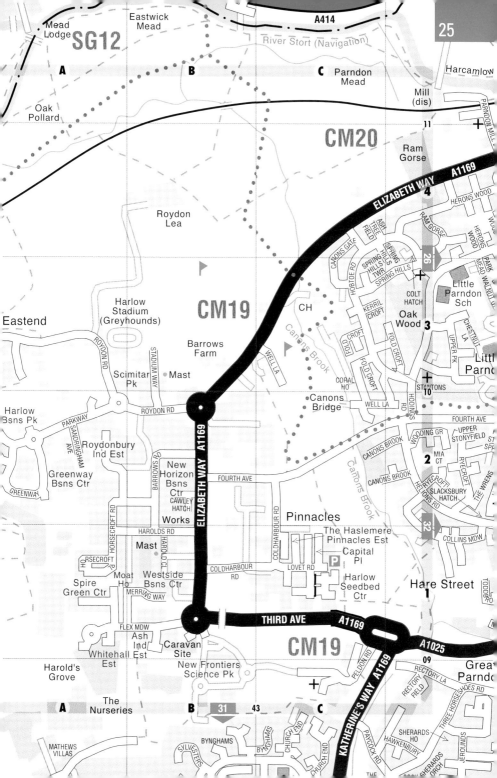

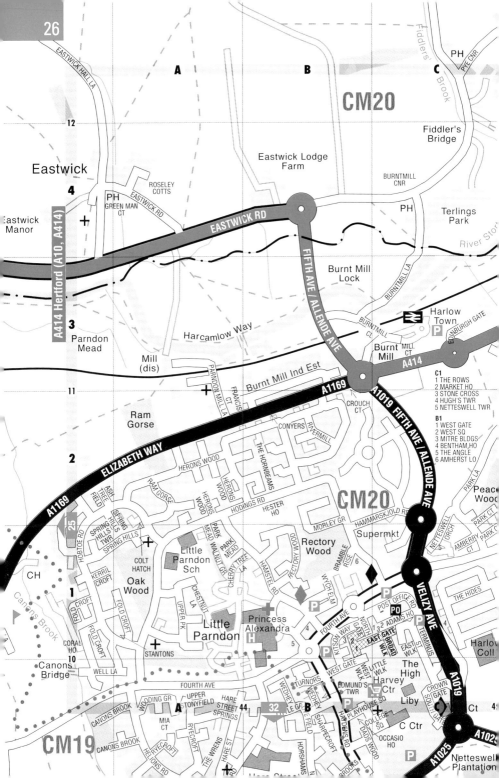

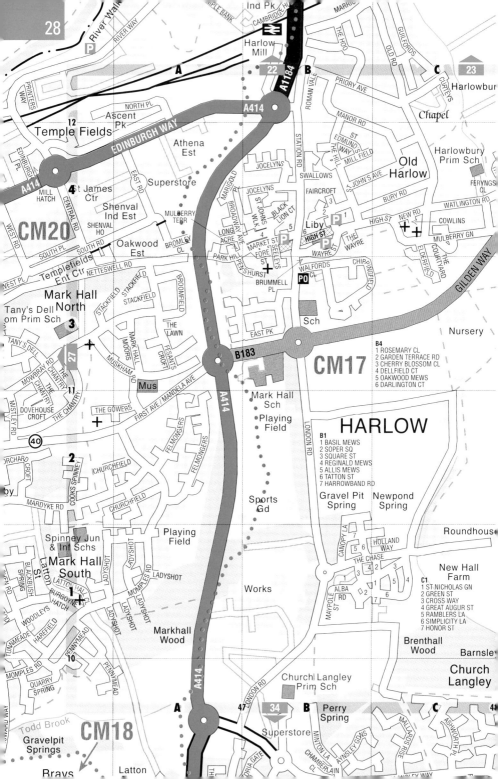

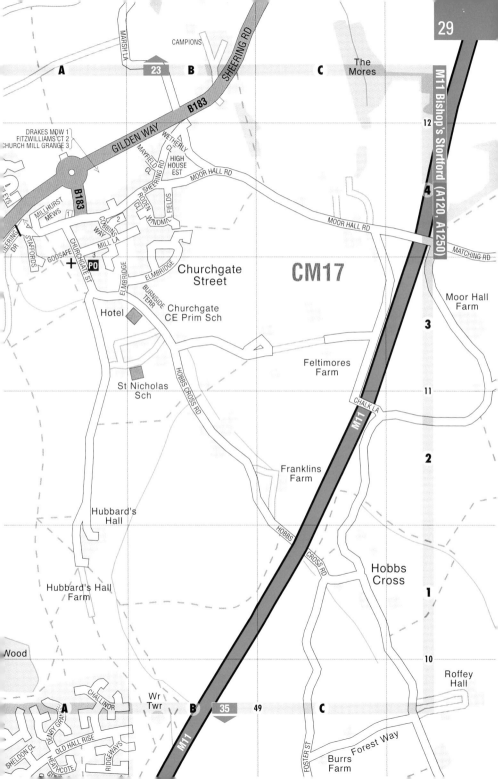

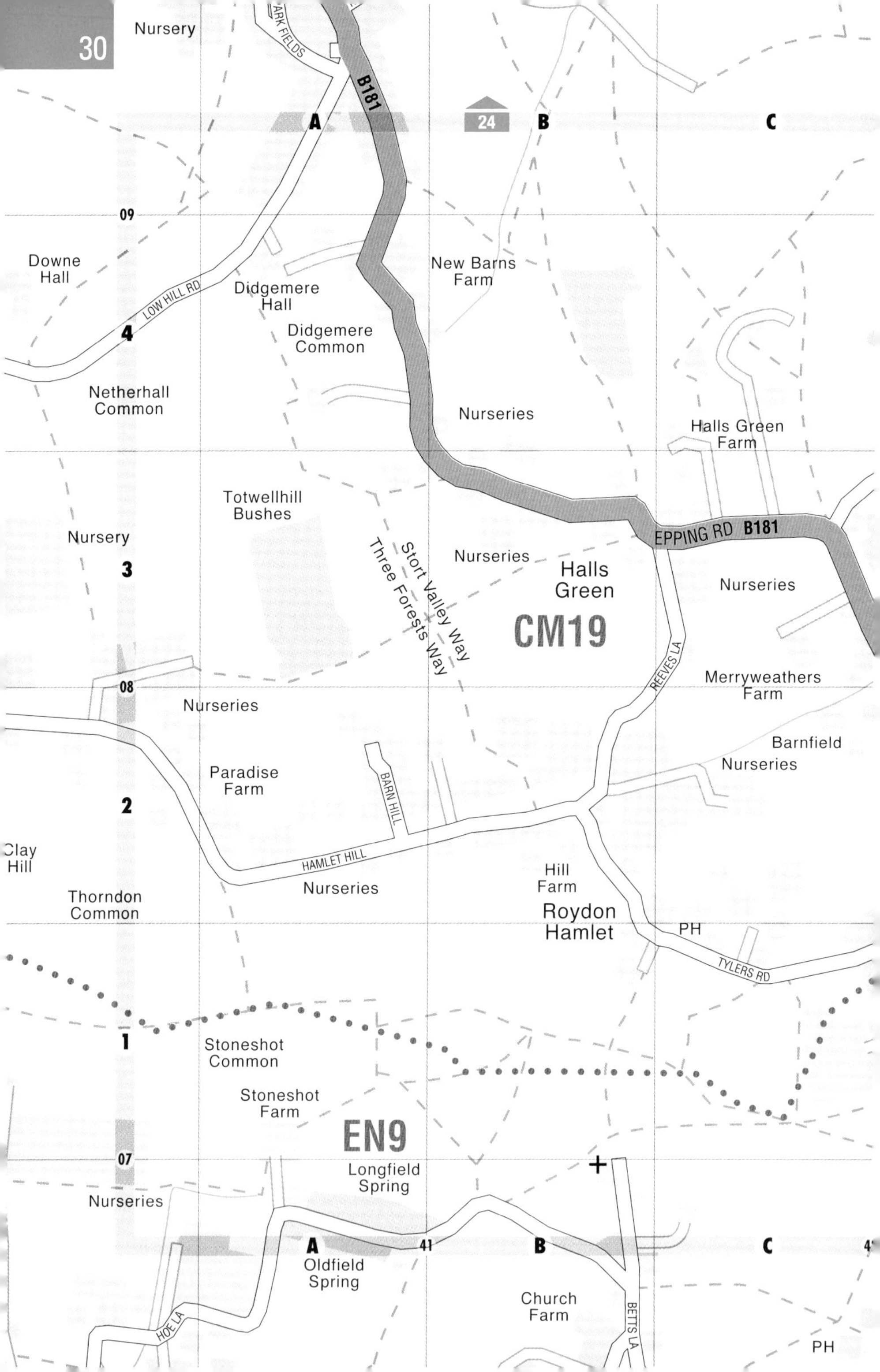

Nursery

PARK FIELDS

B181

09

Downe
Hall

LOW HILL RD

Didgemere
Hall

New Barns
Farm

4

Didgemere
Common

Netherhall
Common

Nurseries

Halls Green
Farm

Totwellhill
Bushes

Nursery

3

Stort Valley Way

Three Forests Way

Nurseries

Halls
Green

CM19

EPPING RD **B181**

Nurseries

REEVES LA

Merryweathers
Farm

08

Nurseries

Barnfield
Nurseries

Paradise
Farm

2

BARN HILL

HAMLET HILL

Clay
Hill

Nurseries

Hill
Farm

Thorndon
Common

**Roydon
Hamlet**

PH

TYLERS RD

1

Stoneshot
Common

Stoneshot
Farm

EN9

07

Longfield
Spring

Nurseries

+

A 41 **B** **C** 4

Oldfield
Spring

BETTS LA

HOE LA

Church
Farm

PH

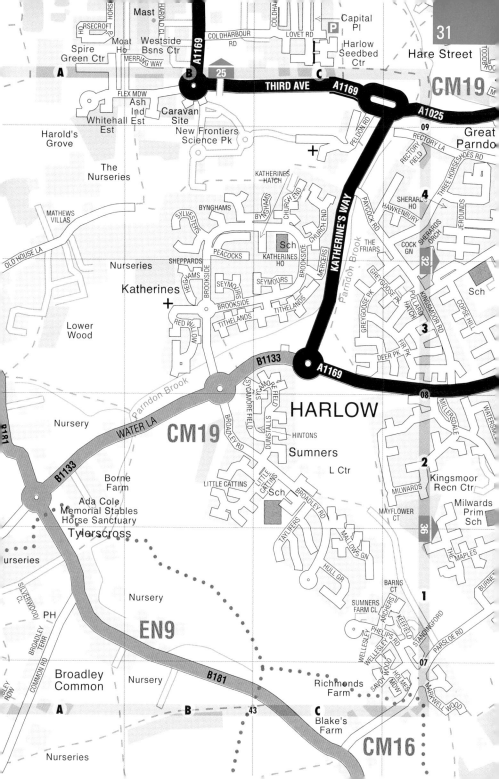

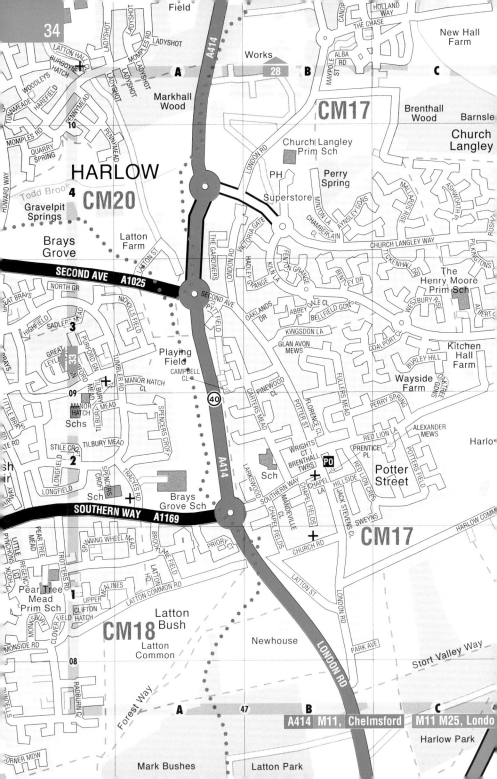

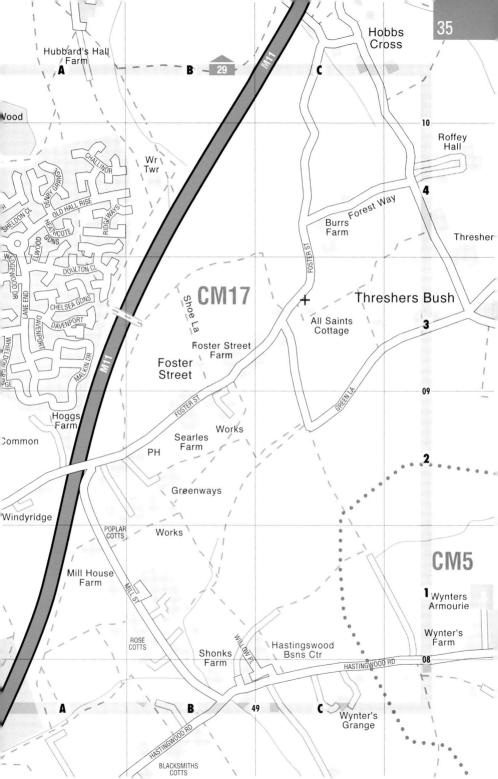

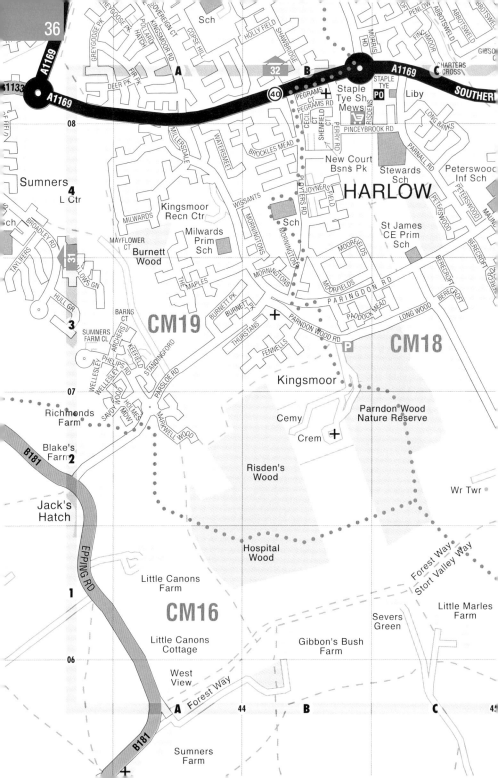

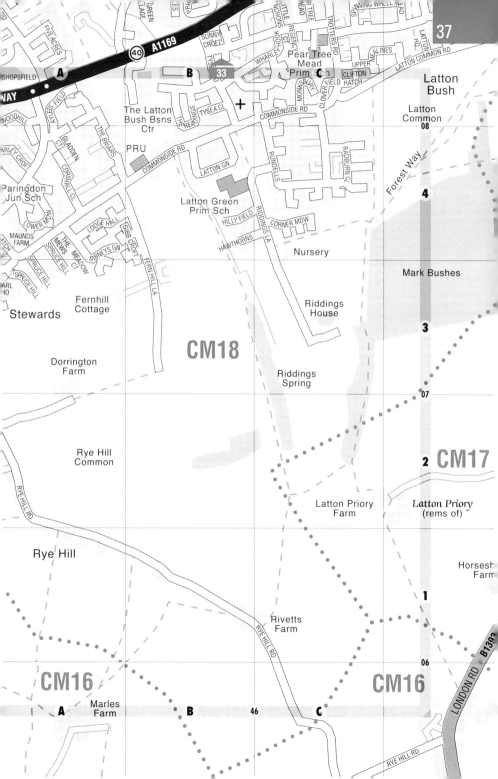

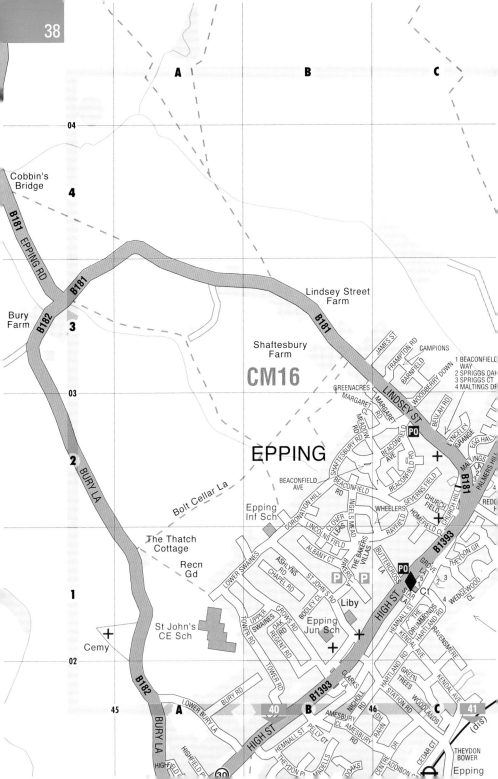

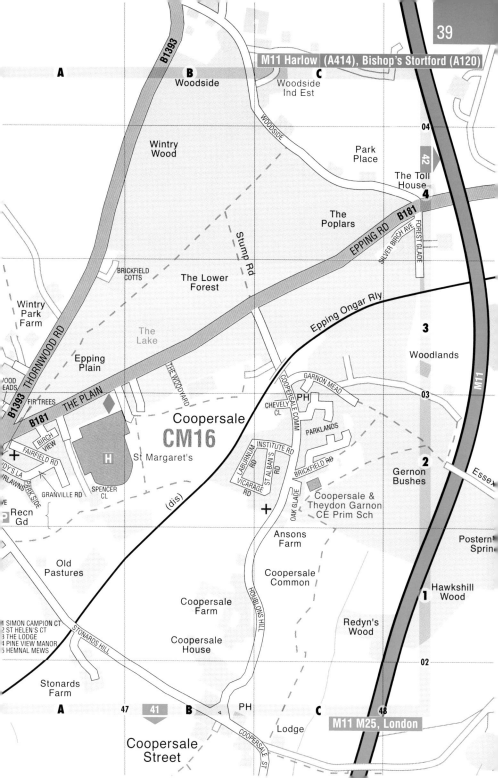

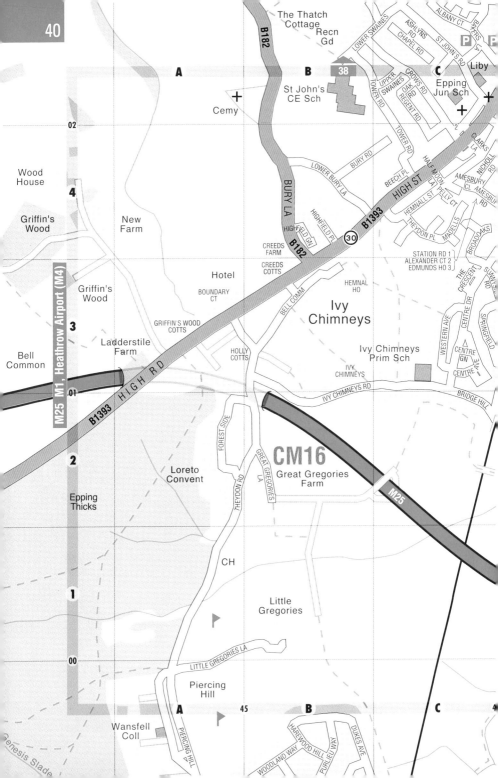

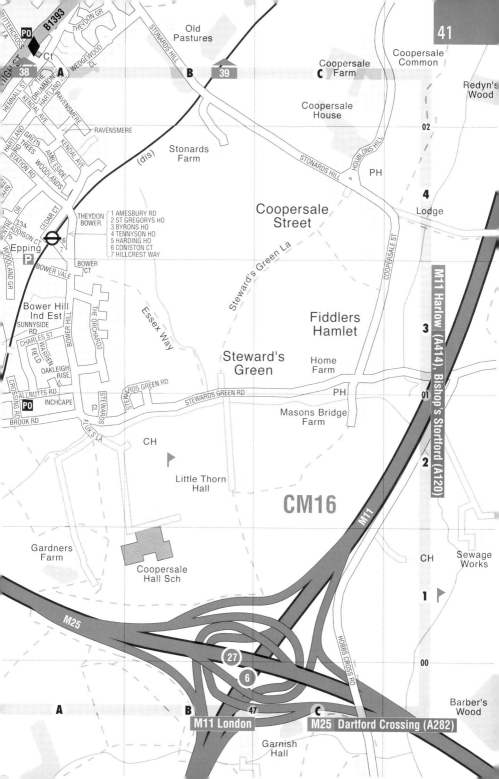

PO
B1393
TTERCROSS LA
HIGH CT LA
Ct
THE KENDRUM
HEMNALL ST
THEYDON GR
WEDGEWOOD CL
STONARDS HILL
Old Pastures

Coopersale Common

Coopersale Farm

Redyn's Wood

38 A B 39 C

HARTLAND
RAVENSMERE
THE DRUMMON
Coopersale House

02

RAVENSMERE
HARTLAND GREEN
RD TREES
KENDAL AVE
AMBLESIDE
WOODLANDS
KENDAL AVE

STATION RD

(dis)
Stonards Farm

STONARDS HILL
HOUBLONS HILL
PH

4
Lodge

THEYDON BOWER
CEDAR CT
234
ADDISON CT
NTRE DR
1 AMESBURY RD
2 ST GREGORYS HO
3 BYRONS HO
4 TENNYSON HO
5 HARDING HO
6 CONISTON CT
7 HILLCREST WAY

Coopersale Street

COOPERSALE ST

Epping
P
BOWER VALE
BOWER CT

Steward's Green La

Fiddlers Hamlet

M11 Harlow (A414), Bishop's Stortford (A120)

3

Bower Hill Ind Est
SUNNYSIDE RD
CHARLES ST
WARREN FIELD
OAKLEIGH RISE
ALLNUTTS RD
CROSSING BROOK ST
THE ORCHARDS
BOWER HILL

Essex Way

Steward's Green

Home Farm

01

PO
INCHCAPE
BROOK RD

STEWARDS CL
STEWARDS GREEN RD
STEWARDS GREEN RD

PH

Masons Bridge Farm

2

FLUX'S LA
CH

Little Thorn Hall

CM16

M11

Gardners Farm

Coopersale Hall Sch

CH

Sewage Works

1

M25

00

M25
27
6

Barber's Wood

A B M11 London 47 C M25 Dartford Crossing (A282)

Garnish Hall

HOBBS CROSS RD

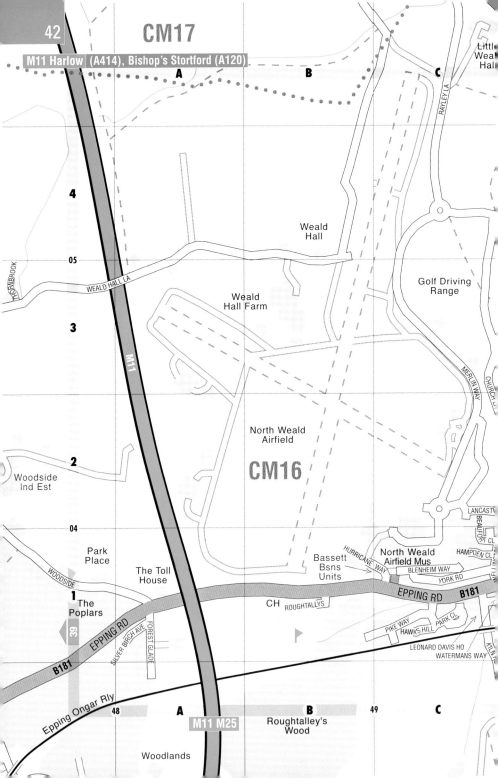

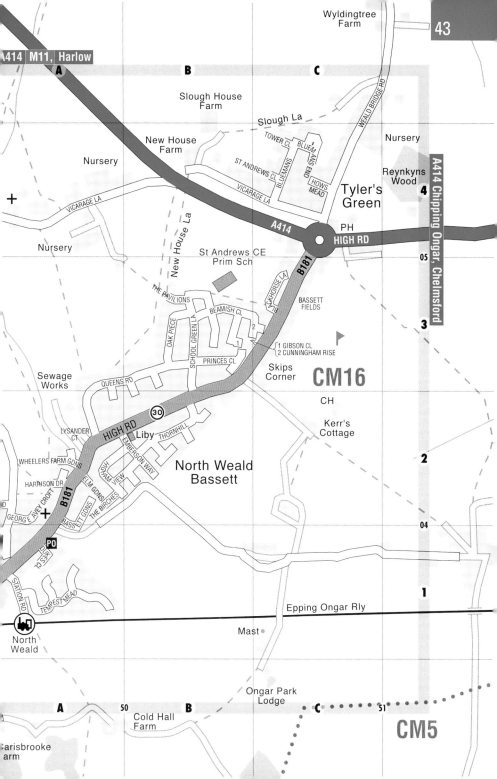

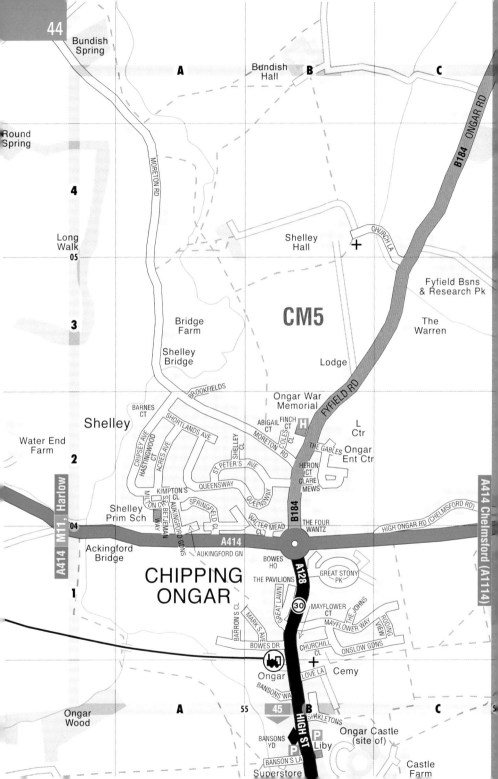

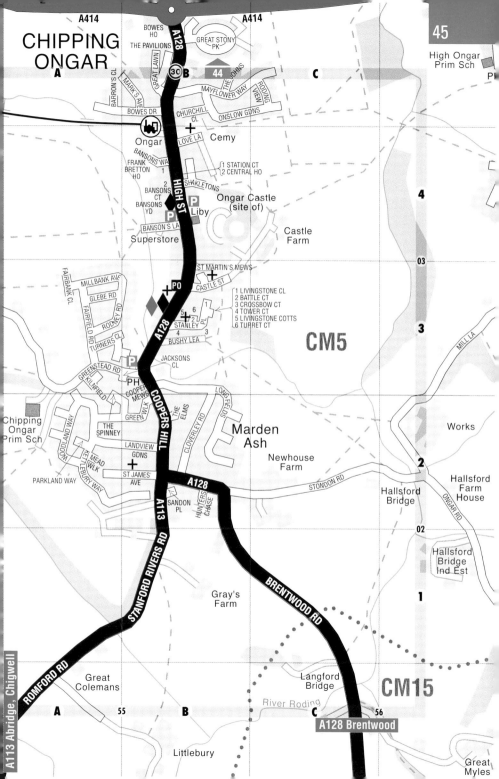

Index

Street names are listed alphabetically and show the locality, the Postcode district, the page number and a reference to the square in which the name falls on the map page

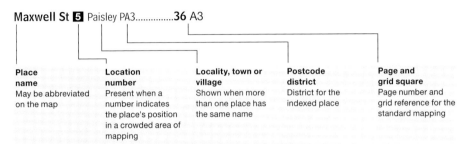

Maxwell St **5** Paisley PA3...............**36** A3

Place name	Location number	Locality, town or village	Postcode district	Page and grid square
May be abbreviated on the map	Present when a number indicates the place's position in a crowded area of mapping	Shown when more than one place has the same name	District for the indexed place	Page number and grid reference for the standard mapping

Towns and villages are listed in CAPITAL LETTERS
Public and commercial buildings are highlighted in **magenta**. **Places of interest** are highlighted in blue with a star *

Abbreviations used in the index

Acad	**Academy**	Ct	**Court**	Hts	**Heights**	Pl	**Place**
App	**Approach**	Ctr	**Centre**	Ind	**Industrial**	Prec	**Precinct**
Arc	**Arcade**	Ctry	**Country**	Inst	**Institute**	Prom	**Promenade**
Ave	**Avenue**	Cty	**County**	Int	**International**	Rd	**Road**
Bglw	**Bungalow**	Dr	**Drive**	Intc	**Interchange**	Recn	**Recreation**
Bldg	**Building**	Dro	**Drove**	Junc	**Junction**	Ret	**Retail**
Bsns, Bus	**Business**	Ed	**Education**	L	**Leisure**	Sh	**Shopping**
Bvd	**Boulevard**	Emb	**Embankment**	La	**Lane**	Sq	**Square**
Cath	**Cathedral**	Est	**Estate**	Liby	**Library**	St	**Street**
Cir	**Circus**	Ex	**Exhibition**	Mdw	**Meadow**	Sta	**Station**
Cl	**Close**	Gd	**Ground**	Meml	**Memorial**	Terr	**Terrace**
Cnr	**Corner**	Gdn	**Garden**	Mkt	**Market**	TH	**Town Hall**
Coll	**College**	Gn	**Green**	Mus	**Museum**	Univ	**University**
Com	**Community**	Gr	**Grove**	Orch	**Orchard**	Wk, Wlk	**Walk**
Comm	**Common**	H	**Hall**	Pal	**Palace**	Wr	**Water**
Cott	**Cottage**	Ho	**House**	Par	**Parade**	Yd	**Yard**
Cres	**Crescent**	Hospl	**Hospital**	Pas	**Passage**		
Cswy	**Causeway**	HQ	**Headquarters**	Pk	**Park**		

Index of towns, villages, streets, hospitals, industrial estates, railway stations, schools, shopping centres, universities and places of interest

Abb–ARD

A

Abbey Dale Cl CM17 . . . . 34 B3
Abbotsweld CM18 . . . . . . 32 C1
Abbotsweld Prim Sch
CM18 . . . . 32 C2
Abbotts Way CM23 . . . . . 13 A1
Abercrombie Way CM18,
CM19 . . . . 32 B2
Abigail Ct CM5 . . . . 44 B2
Acorn Mews CM18 . . . . . 33 C2
Acres Ave CM5 . . . . 44 A2

Ada Cole Meml Stables
Horse Sanctuary*
CM19 . . . . 31 A2
Adams Ho CM20 . . . . 26 C1
Adderley Rd CM23 . . . . . 11 B1
Addison Ct CM16 . . . . . . 41 A4
Adingtons CM20 . . . . 27 B2
Airey Hos CO10 . . . . 28 C1
Albany Ct CM16 . . . . 38 B1
Alba Rd CM17 . . . . 28 B1
Albert Gdns CM17 . . . . . 34 C3
Alconbury CM23 . . . . 5 A1
Alcorns The CM24 . . . . . 4 B3
Alderbury Rd CM24 . . . . . 4 B4
Alder Cl CM23 . . . . 12 C2
Alders Wlk CM21 . . . . . . 19 A2

Alexander Ct CM16 . . . . . 40 C4
Alexander Mews CM17 . 34 C2
Allen Ho CM21 . . . . 19 B2
Allis Mews **5** CM17 . . . . 28 B1
Allnutts Rd CM16 . . . . . . 41 A2
All Saints CE Prim Sch
CM23 . . . . 14 A4
All Saints Cl
Ashdon CB10 . . . . 33 B3
Bishop's Stortford CM23 . 11 C2
Alpha Pl **4** CM23 . . . . . . 11 B2
Alsa Gdns CM22 . . . . 3 B3
Alsa Leys CM22 . . . . 3 B3
Altham Gr CM20 . . . . 27 B3
Amberry Ct CM20 . . . . . 26 C1
Ambleside CM16 . . . . . . 41 A4

Amesbury Cl CM16 . . . . . 40 C4
Amesbury Rd CM16 . . . . 40 C4
Amherst Lo **6** CM20 . . . 26 B1
Anchor St CM23 . . . . 13 C4
Anglesey Cl CM23 . . . . . 10 B1
Angle The **5** CM20 . . . . 26 B1
Appleton Cl CM19 . . . . . 32 B3
Appleton Fields CM23 . . 13 A2
April Pl CM21 . . . . 19 B3
Apsley Cl CM23 . . . . 13 B2
Apton Ct CM23 . . . . 11 B1
Apton Fields **7** CM23 . . 13 B4
Apton Rd CM23 . . . . 11 B1
Archers CM19 . . . . 36 A3
Ardley Cres CM22 . . . . . 21 C3
ARDLEY END 21 C2

Arkwrights CM20. . . . . . .27 B1
Armourers Cl CM23 . . . .12 A2
Ascent Pk CM20. . . . . . . .22 B1
Ascot Cl CM23 . . . . .14 B4
Ashby Rise CM23 . . . . .5 A1
Ashdale CM23 . . . . .12 C2
Ashdon Mus The*
 CB10 . . . . .34 A4
Ashdon Rd CB10 . . . . . . .36 B3
Ashdon Road Commercial
 Ctr CB10. . . . . .31 C1
ASHEN 28 C1
Ashen Cl CO10 . . . . .28 C1
Ashen Hill CO10. . . . . . . .28 B2
Ashen La CO10. . . . . .28 B3
Ashen Rd CO10 . . . . .29 C1
Ash Groves CM21 . . . . . .19 C2
Ash Ind Est CM19 . . . . . .25 B1
Ashlyns Rd CM16. . . . . . .38 B1
Ash Tree Field CM20. . . .25 C4
Ashworth Pl CM17 . . . . .34 C4
Aspens The CM23 . . . . . . .5 A3
Aspin Mews CB10 . . . . . .31 A1
Aster Cl CM23. . . . . .12 C4
Astra Ctr CM20. . . . . . . .27 B4
Athena Est CM20. . . . . . .28 A4
Atherton End CM21 . . . .19 A3
Audrey Gdns CM23 . . . . .13 B2
Aukingford Gdns CM5 . .44 A2
Aukingford Gn CM5 . . . .44 A1
Avenue Pl CM23. . . . . . . .13 C4
Avenue Rd CM23 . . . . . . .14 A2
Aylets Field CM18 . . . . . .33 A1
Aynsley Gdns CM17 . . . .34 B4
Aynsworth Ave CM23 . . . .5 A2

B

Back La
 Ickleton CB10 . . . . .21 B4
 Little Hallingbury CM22. . . . 2 A2
Badgers CM23 . . . . .13 A3
Bakers Ct 5 CM23 . . . . . .11 C1
Bakers La CM16. . . . . . . .38 B1
Bakers Villas The CM16 .38 B1
Bakers Wlk CM11 . . . . . .19 A2
Bakery Cl CM19 . . . . .24 B2
Bakery Ct CM24 . . . . .4 A2
Bansons Ct CM5 . . . . . . .45 B4
Banson's La CM5. . . . . . .45 B4
Bansons Way CM5 . . . . .45 B4
Bansons Yd CM5 . . . . . . .45 B4
Barkers Mead CM22 . . . . .2 A3
Barley Croft CM18. . . . . .37 A4
Barley Hills CM23 . . . . . .13 A2
Barnard Rd CM21 . . . . . .19 A4
Barnes Ct CM5. . . . . .44 A2
Barnfield CM16 . . . . .38 C3
Barn Hill CM19. . . . . .30 A2
Barn Mead CM18. . . . . . .33 A2
Barns Ct CM19 . . . . .36 A3
Barons The CM23. . . . . . .12 C3

Barrells Down Rd
 CM23 . . . . .11 A3
Barrett La 5 CM23 . . . . .11 B1
Barron's Cl CM5 . . . . . . .44 A1
Barrows Rd CM19 . . . . . .25 B2
Bartholomew Rd 8
 CM23 . . . . .13 B4
Basbow La 2 CM23 . . . .11 B1
Basil Mews 1 CM17. . . . .28 B1
Bassett Bsns Units
 CM16 . . . . .42 B1
Bassett Fields CM16. . . .43 C3
Bassett Gdns CM16. . . . .43 A2
Bassingbourn Rd CM24. . .8 C3
Battle Ct CM5 . . . . .45 B3
Beaconfield Ave CM16. .38 C2
Beaconfield Rd CM16. . .38 C2
Beaconfield Way CM16 .38 C2
Beadles The CM22. . . . . . .2 A3
Beamish Cl CM16 . . . . . .43 B3
Beaufort Cl CM16 . . . . . .42 C1
Beaumont Park Dr
 CM19 . . . . .24 A2
Bedwell Rd CM22 . . . . . . .3 A4
Beech Cl CM22. . . . . .17 A4
Beech Dr CM21 . . . . .22 C4
Beechfield CM21. . . . . . . .19 B2
Beechlands CM23 . . . . . .13 B3
Beech Pl CM16. . . . . .40 C4
Beehive Ct CM22. . . . . . .21 B4
Beldams Gate CM23 . . . .14 B2
Beldams La CM23 . . . . . .14 A1
Belgrave Ho 6 CM23. . .14 A4
Bell Comm CM16. . . . . . .40 B3
Bellfield Gdns CM17. . . .34 B3
Bell Mead CM21. . . . . . . .19 A2
Bells Hill CM23. . . . . .11 A1
Bell St CM21. . . . . .19 A2
Bells Wlk CM21 . . . . .19 A2
Belmer Rd CM24 . . . . .7 C4
Bench Barn Farm CO10 23 C3
Benhooks Ave CM23. . . .13 A4
Benhooks Pl 1 CM23 . .13 A3
Bentfield End Cswy
 CM24 . . . . .4 A3
Bentfield Gdns CM24 . . . .4 A4
BENTFIELD GREEN 4 A4
Bentfield Pl CM24. . . . . . .4 A3
Bentfield Prim Sch
 CM24 . . . . .4 A4
Bentfield Rd CM24 . . . . . .4 A3
Bentham Ho 4 CM20. . .26 B1
Bentley Cl CM23 . . . . . . .13 B3
Bentley Dr CM17 . . . . . . .34 B3
Bentleys CM22 . . . . .21 C3
Bentley Villas CM22 . . . .21 C3
Berecroft CM18 . . . . .36 C3
Betjeman Way CM5 . . . .44 A2
Beulah Rd CM16 . . . . . . .38 C2
Birchalls CM24. . . . . .4 B4
BIRCHANGER 6 A2
Birchanger CE Prim Sch
 CM23 . . . . .5 C2

Birchanger Ind Est
 CM23 . . . . .5 A2
Birchanger La CM23. . . . .5 C2
Birches The CM16 . . . . . .43 A2
Birch View CM16 . . . . . . .39 A2
Birchwood CM23. . . . . . . .5 C2
Birchwood High Sch
 CM23 . . . . .14 B4
Birds Cl CB10 . . . . .21 B4
Bishop's Ave CM23 . . . . .13 B1
Bishopsfield CM18 . . . . .33 A1
BISHOP'S PARK 12 A4
Bishops Park Way
 CM23 . . . . .10 A1
BISHOP'S
 STORTFORD. 10 C1
Bishop's Stortford Bsns
 Ctr CM23 . . . . .13 C4
Bishop's Stortford Coll
 CM23 . . . . .11 A1
Bishop's Stortford High
 Sch The CM23. . . . . . . .13 B2
Bishop's Stortford Mus*
 CM23 . . . . .13 C4
Bishop's Stortford Sta
 CM23 . . . . .13 C4
Blackbushe CM23 . . . . . . .5 B1
Blackbush Spring
 CM20. . . . . .27 C1
Blackhorse La CM16. . . .43 C3
Black Lion Ct CM17. . . . .28 B4
Blacksmiths Cl CM23 . . .12 A3
Blacksmiths Hill CO10. .38 A4
Blacksmiths Way CM21 18 A1
Blair Cl CM23 . . . . .10 B1
Blakes Ct CM21 . . . . .19 A2
Blenheim Cl CM11 . . . . .22 C4
Blenheim Ct CM23 . . . . .10 B1
Blenheim Way CM16 . . .42 C1
Blois Rd CB9. . . . . .25 B3
Bluemans CM16. . . . . . . .43 C4
Bluemans End CM16 . . .43 C4
Blythwood Gdns CM24.. .4 A2
Bodley Cl CM16 . . . . .38 B1
Bonks Hill CM21 . . . . . . .18 C1
Boreham Pl CO9 . . . . . . .26 A2
Boundary Cl CM23 . . . . .13 C3
Boundary Ct CM16 . . . . .40 A3
Boundary Rd CM23. . . . .13 C3
Bourne The CM23 . . . . . .11 C2
Bower Ct CM16 . . . . .41 A3
Bower Hill CM16 . . . . . . .41 A3
Bower Hill Ind Est
 CM16. . . . . .41 A3
Bower Vale CM16. . . . . . .41 A3
Bowes Dr CM5 . . . . .44 B1
Bowes Ho CM5. . . . . .44 B1
Bowling Cl 14 CM23 . . .13 A4
Boyd Cl 1 CM23 . . . . . . .14 A4
Bradley Comm CM23 . . . .5 B3
Braggon's Hill IP29 . . . . .2 A3
Bramble Rise CM20 . . . .26 B1
Brambles The CM23 . . . .12 B4
BRAYS GROVE 33 C4

Brays Grove Sch CM18. .34 A2
Brays Mead CM18. . . . . .33 B2
Braziers Quay CM23. . . .13 C4
Brenthall Twrs CM17 . . .34 B2
Brentwood Rd CM5,
 CM15. . . . . .45 C1
Brewers Cl CM23. . . . . . .12 B3
BREWER'S END 16 C3
Brewery La CM24 . . . . . . .4 B3
Brewery Yd CM24 . . . . . . .4 B3
Briars The CM18 . . . . . . .37 A4
Brickfield Cotts CM16 . .39 A4
Brickfield Rd CM16. . . . .39 C2
Bridewell Ind Est CO10 .20 A1
Bridewell St CO10. . . . . .20 A1
Bridge Cotts CO10 . . . . .18 C2
Bridgeford Ho 13 CM23 13 B4
Bridge Hill CM16. . . . . . .40 C2
Bridge St CM23 . . . . .11 B1
Britannia Pl 3 CM23. . .13 A3
Broadfield
 Bishop's Stortford
 CM23 . . . . .11 B4
 Harlow CM20. . . . . .27 A1
Broadfield Rd CM22 . . . .17 C3
Broadfields CM21 . . . . . .18 A1
Broadfields Prim Sch
 CM20. . . . . .27 A1
Broadleaf Ave CM23. . . .12 C2
Broadley Rd CM19. . . . . .31 C2
Broadley Terr EN9. . . . . .31 A1
Broadoaks CM16 . . . . . . .40 C4
Broadway Ave CM17. . . .28 A4
Broad Wlk CM20 . . . . . . .26 C1
Brockles Mead CM19 . . .36 B4
Bromley Cl CM20. . . . . . .28 A4
Brook Cotts CM24. . . . . . .4 B1
Brooke Gdns CM23 . . . . .14 B3
Brook End CM21 . . . . . . .18 C2
Brook Farm Cl CM23 . . .12 B1
Brookfields
 Chipping Ongar CM5 . . . . .44 A3
 Sawbridgeworth CM21 . . .18 C2
Brookhouse Pl 3
 CM23 . . . . .11 B2
Brook La CM21. . . . . .18 C2
Brooklane Field CM18 . .34 A1
Brook Rd
 Epping CM16 . . . . .41 A2
 Sawbridgeworth CM21 . . .19 A1
 Stansted Mountfitchet
 CM24 . . . . .4 B2
Brookside CM19 . . . . . . .31 C3
Brook St CO10 . . . . .2 A1
BROOK STREET 2 A1
Brook View CM24. . . . . . . .4 B1
Broom Farm Rd CM22 . . .3 B3
Broomfield CM20 . . . . . . .28 A3
Broomfields CM22 . . . . .21 B4
Brummell Pl CM17 . . . . .28 B3
Bryan Rd CM23 . . . . .11 B2
Buckenhoe Rd CB10. . . .31 A1

Bullfields CM21 . . . . .19 A3
Burghley Ave CM23. . . . . .10 B1
Burgoyne Hatch CM20. .27 C1
Burley Hill CM17 . . . . . . .34 C3
Burley Rd CM23 . . . . .13 C2
Burnells Way CM24. . . . . 4 B3
Burnett Pk CM19. . . . . . . .36 A3
Burnside CM21 . . . . .18 C2
Burnside Terr CM17 . . . . .29 B3
Burntmill Cl CM20. . . . . .26 B3
Burntmill Cnr CM20 . . . .26 C4
Burnt Mill Comp Sch
  CM20. . . . . .27 A2
Burnt Mill Ind Est
  CM20. . . . . .26 B3
Burntmill La CM20 . . . . .26 C3
BURTON END 7 B4
Burtons Mill CM21 . . . . .19 B3
Bury Lodge La CM24. . . . . 6 C2
Bury Rd
  Epping CM16 . . . . .40 B4
  Harlow CM17. . . . . .28 C4
Bushey Croft CM18 . . . . .33 A3
BUSH FAIR 33 C2
Bush Fair CM18 . . . . .33 B2
Bush Ho CM18 . . . . .33 B2
Bushy Lea CM5 . . . . .45 B3
Butler's Hall La CM23 . .12 A1
Butlers La CB10. . . . . . . .32 B1
Buttercross La CM16 . . .38 C1
Buttersweet Rise CM21 19 A1
Bylands Cl CM23 . . . . . . .12 C4
Bynghams CM19 . . . . . . .31 B4
Byrd's Farm La CB10 . . .31 A1
Byrons Ho CM16 . . . . . . .41 A4

C

Callis Ct CO10 . . . . .20 A1
Calverley Cl CM23. . . . . .13 A2
Cambridge Cotts CM22 16 C3
Cambridge Ho CM17 . . .22 C1
Cambridge Rd
  Harlow CM20. . . . . .22 C2
  Sawbridgeworth CM21 . .19 A4
  Stansted Mountfitchet
    CM24 . . . . 4 B4
Campbell Cl CM17 . . . . .34 A3
Campions
  Epping CM16 . . . . .38 C3
  Harlow CM17. . . . . .23 C1
Campions The CM24. . . . . 4 B4
Canfield CM23 . . . . .11 A2
Canfield Dr CM22 . . . . . .17 C2
Canfield Rd CM22 . . . . . .17 B1
Cannons Cl CM23 . . . . . .11 C3
Cannons Mead CM24 . . . 4 A3
Cannons Mill La CM23 . .11 C3
Canons Brook CM19. . . .32 A4
Canons Gate CM20 . . . . .25 C4
Canopy La CM17 . . . . . . .28 B1
Capital Pl CM19 . . . . . . .25 C1

Careless Ct **21** CM23. . . .11 B1
Carl Ho CM18 . . . . .37 A3
Carpenters The CM23. . .12 A3
Carrigans CM23. . . . . . . .11 A2
Carters Leys CM23 . . . . .10 C2
Carters Mead CM17 . . . .34 B2
Castle St
  Bishop's Stortford
    CM23 . . . . .13 B4
  Chipping Ongar CM5 . . . . .45 B3
Castle View CM23 . . . . . .11 C1
Castle Wlk CM24. . . . . . . 4 B2
Causeway The
  1 Bishop's Stortford
    CM23 . . . . .11 C1
  Henham CB11 . . . . .41 B3
Cavell Ct CM23. . . . . .14 A2
Cavell Dr CM23 . . . . .14 A2
CAVENDISH. 18 B1
Cavendish CE Prim Sch
  CO10 . . . . .18 B2
Cavendish La CO10. . . . .19 B3
Cawkell Cl CM24 . . . . 4 A3
Cawley Hatch CM19 . . . .25 B2
Cecil Cl CM23. . . . . .14 C3
Cecil Ct CM18. . . . . .32 B1
Cedar Cl CM21 . . . . .19 A1
Cedar Ct
  Bishop's Stortford
    CM23 . . . . .11 B3
  Epping CM16 . . . . .41 A4
Cedar Pk CM23 . . . . .12 C2
Cedars The CM24. . . . . . . 4 A2
Cedarwood Ct CM18. . . .33 B2
Cemetery Rd CM23. . . . .13 B4
Central Ho CM5. . . . . . . .45 B4
Central Rd CM20 . . . . . . .27 C4
Centre Ave CM16. . . . . . .40 C3
Centre Dr CM16. . . . . . . .40 C3
Centre Gn CM16 . . . . . . .40 C3
Chalk La CM17 . . . . .29 C2
Chalklands CB10. . . . . . .31 A1
Chalks Ave CM21. . . . . . .18 C3
Challinor CM17 . . . . .35 A4
Chamberlain Cl CM17 . .34 B4
Chandlers Cl CM23 . . . . .12 B2
Chantry Cl CM23 . . . . . . .11 A2
Chantry Mount CM23. . .11 A2
Chantry Rd CM23. . . . . . .11 A2
Chantry The
  6 Bishop's Stortford
    CM23 . . . . .11 B2
  Harlow CM20. . . . . .27 C2
CHAPELEND 25 C2
Chapel Fields
  Harlow CM17. . . . . .34 B2
  Takeley CM22 . . . . .16 C3
Chapel Hill CM24. . . . . . . 4 B2
Chapel La CM17. . . . . . . .34 B2
Chapel Rd CM16 . . . . . . .38 B1
Chapel Row **3** CM23 . . .13 B4
Chapel St CO10 . . . . .27 C3
Charles St CM16 . . . . . . .41 A3
Charters Cross CM18 . . .32 C1

Chartwell Pl CM23 . . . . . .5 A1
Chase The
  Bishop's Stortford
    CM23 . . . . .13 B4
  Harlow CM17. . . . . .28 B1
Chaseways CM21. . . . . . .22 C4
Chatsworth Cl CM23. . . .10 B1
Chelsea Gdns CM17 . . . .35 A3
Chenies Gn CM23 . . . . . .12 C4
Chequers CM23 . . . . .10 B2
Chequers La CO10 . . . . . . 2 B1
Cherry Blossom Cl **8**
  CM17 . . . . .28 B4
Cherry Gdns
  Bishop's Stortford
    CM23 . . . . .11 C2
  Sawbridgeworth CM21 . .19 A4
Cherry Tree La CM20 . . .26 A1
Chesfield Cl CM23. . . . . .13 B3
Chestnut Cl CM23. . . . . .13 A4
Chestnut Dr CM22. . . . . .21 A4
Chestnut La CM20. . . . . .26 A1
Chestnut Way CM22 . . . .17 A3
Chevely Cl CM16 . . . . . . .39 C2
Chinnery Hill CM23. . . . .13 B3
Chippingfield CM17 . . . .28 B3
CHIPPING ONGAR 44 A1
Chipping Ongar Prim Sch
  CM5. . . . . .45 A2
Christian Sch The
  CM22. . . . . .16 C3
Church Cl CO10 . . . . .18 C2
Church Cres CM21 . . . . .19 B2
CHURCH END 33 C3
Church End CM19 . . . . . .31 C4
Churchfield CM20. . . . . .28 A2
Church Field
  Ashdon CB10. . . . . .33 B3
  Epping CM16 . . . . .38 C2
Churchfields CM24. . . . . . 4 C2
Churchgate CE Prim Sch
  CM17. . . . . .29 B3
Churchgate St CM17 . . .29 A4
CHURCHGATE STREET 29 B3
Church Hill
  Ashdon CB10. . . . . .33 B3
  Epping CM16 . . . . .38 C2
Churchill Cl CM5. . . . . . .44 B1
Churchill Cnr CM24 . . . . . 4 C1
Church La
  Bishop's Stortford
    CM23 . . . . .12 C1
  Chipping Ongar CM5 . . . .44 C4
  Debden CB11. . . . . .41 A3
  North Weald Bassett
    CM16 . . . . .42 C3
  Takeley, Brewer's End
    CM22. . . . . .16 C3
CHURCH LANGLEY 34 C4
Church Langley Com Prim
  Sch CM17. . . . . .34 B4
Church Langley Way
  CM17. . . . . .34 C4
Church Leys CM18 . . . . .33 B3

Church Manor CM23 . . .14 A4
Church Mead CM19 . . . .24 A3
Church Mill Grange
  CM17. . . . . .29 A4
Church Pk CO10 . . . . . . .28 B3
Church Rd
  Harlow CM17. . . . . .34 B1
  Stansted Mountfitchet
    CM24 . . . . 4 C1
Church St
  Bishop's Stortford
    CM23 . . . . .11 B1
  Sawbridgeworth CM21 . .19 A2
Church Terr CO10 . . . . . .26 C2
Church View CO10. . . . . .26 C3
Church Wlk CM21 . . . . . .19 B2
CLARE. 20 A1
Clare Mews CM5 . . . . . . .44 B2
Clare Mid Sch CO10 . . . .20 A1
Clarence Rd CM24 . . . . . 4 B3
Clarendon Rd CM6 . . . . .17 C3
Clarks La CM16 . . . . .40 C4
Clayponds CM23 . . . . . . .14 A3
Clifford Ct **9** CM23. . . . .11 C1
Clifton Hatch CM18 . . . .33 C1
Clipped Hedge CM22 . . .21 C4
Close The
  Debden CB11. . . . . .41 B3
  Hatfield Heath CM22. . . .21 B4
Clover Ave CM23 . . . . . . .12 A4
Clover Field CM18. . . . . .33 C1
Clover Leas CM16 . . . . . .38 B2
Cloverley Rd CM5 . . . . . .45 B2
Cluanie Orch CO10 . . . . .19 A1
Coalport Cl CM17 . . . . . .34 C3
Cobbins Way CM17. . . . .29 A4
Cock Gn CM19 . . . . .32 A2
Coldharbour Rd CM19 . .25 C1
Coles Cl CM5 . . . . .44 B2
College Cl CM23 . . . . . . .10 C1
College Sq CM20. . . . . . .32 C4
COLLINS CROSS. 14 A4
Collins Cross CM23. . . . . .5 A1
Collins Mdw CM19 . . . . .32 A3
Colt Hatch CM20 . . . . . . .26 A1
Coltsfield CM24. . . . . 4 B4
Colts The CM23 . . . . .13 A2
Columbines The CO10 . .19 A2
Colyn Pl CB10. . . . . .31 A1
Commonfields CM20 . . .27 A1
Commonside Rd CM18 . .37 B4
Coney Gree CM21 . . . . . .18 C3
Conifer Ct **7** CM23. . . . .11 B2
Coniston Ct CM16 . . . . . .41 A4
Conyers CM20 . . . . .26 B2
Cooks Spinney CM20 . . .27 C2
COOPERSALE 39 B2
Coopersale Comm
  CM16. . . . . .39 C3
Coopersale Hall Sch
  CM16. . . . . .41 B1
COOPERSALE STREET 41 C4

Coopersale & Theydon Garnon CE Prim Sch
CM16 . . . .**39** C2
Coopers Cl CM23. . . . . . .**12** A2
Coopers End Rd CM24. . . **8** C2
Coopers End Rdbt CM24 **9** A3
Coopers Hill CM5 . . . . . .**45** B2
Coopers Mews CM5 . . . .**45** B3
Coopers Villas CM22. . . . . .**9** A2
Coploe Rd CB10. . . . .**21** B3
Coploe Rise CB10 . . . . . .**21** B4
Copper Ct CM21 . . . .**19** A2
Coppice Hatch CM18 . .**32** C2
Coppice The CM23 . . . . .**12** C3
Copse Hill CM19 . . . .**32** A1
Copse The CM23 . . . .**14** B4
Copshall Cl CM18 . . . . . .**37** A4
Coral Ho CM20. . . . .**25** C3
Corner Ho CM18 . . . .**33** B2
Corner Mdw CM18 . . . . .**37** C4
Corner Pk CB10 . . . .**31** A1
Cornwall Ho CM23 . . . . .**13** A2
Cornwallis Pl CB10. . . . . .**31** A1
Coronation Ho CM16. . . **38** B2
Coronation Rd CM23 . . .**13** A3
Corriander Dr CM22. . . . . . **3** C3
Court Cl CM23 . . . .**13** A3
Courtyard The CM17. . . .**28** C4
Cowlins CM17 . . . .**28** C4
Cox Ley CM22 . . . .**21** B4
Cox's Gdns CM23. . . . . . .**13** A3
Crafton Gn CM24. . . . . **4** B3
Cranbrook La CO10 . . . .**21** A2
Cranmore Cl CM22 . . . . . . **3** B3
Cranmoregreen La
CO10 . . . .**21** A4
Cranwell Gdns CM23 . . . . **5** B1
Creeds Cotts CM16. . . . .**40** B3
Creeds Farm CM16 . . . . .**40** B3
Crescent Rd CM23. . . . . .**13** C4
Crescent The
Epping CM16 . . . .**40** C3
Harlow CM17. . . . .**22** C2
Crest The CM21 . . . .**18** C2
Cricketfield La CM23 . . .**11** A2
Cripsey Ave CM5 . . . .**44** A2
Croasdaile Rd CM24. . . . . . **4** B4
Croasdale Cl CM24 . . . . . . **4** B4
Crocus Fields CB10. . . . .**31** A1
Crofters CM21 . . . .**19** A3
Crofters End CM21 . . . . .**19** A3
Croft The CM22 . . . . **3** B2
Croft Villas CO10 . . . .**20** A4
Cromwell Cl CM23 . . . . .**10** A1
Crossbow Ct CM5 . . . . . .**45** B3
Crossing Rd CM16. . . . . .**41** A2
Cross Way **3** CM17. . . .**28** C1
Crouch Ct CM20. . . . .**26** B3
Crown Cl CM22 . . . .**20** A1
Crownfield Rd CO10. . . . . .**2** A1
Crown Gate CM20 . . . . . .**32** C4
Crown Terr CM23. . . . . . .**11** C1
Crows Rd CM16 . . . .**38** B1
Crozier Ave CM23 . . . . . .**10** B2

Cunningham Rise
CM16 . . . .**43** C3
Curteys CM17 . . . .**23** A1
Cutforth Rd CM21. . . . . .**19** A3
Cutlers Cl CM23. . . . .**12** B3
Cygnet Ct **11** CM23 . . . . .**13** B4

D

Dads Wood CM20 . . . . . .**32** B4
Dale Ct CM21 . . . .**18** C1
Dalhams CO10 . . . .**18** B1
Dalton Gdns CM23 . . . . .**13** A2
Dane Acres CM23 . . . . . .**10** C2
Dane Ho CM23 . . . .**10** C2
Dane O'Coys Rd CM23 . .**11** A3
Dane Pk CM23 . . . .**10** C2
Dane St CM23. . . . .**11** C1
Darlington Ct **6** CM17. .**28** B4
Dashes The CM20 . . . . . .**27** A1
Davenport CM17 . . . .**35** A3
DEBDEN. **41** B3
Debden CE Prim Sch
CB11 . . . .**41** B3
Deer Pk CM19 . . . .**32** A1
Dellfield Ct **4** CM17. . . .**28** B4
Dell La
Bishop's Stortford, Hockerill
CM23 . . . .**11** C1
Little Hallingbury CM22. . . . .**2** A4
Dells The **11** CM23. . . . . .**11** B1
De Mandeville Rd CM22 . **3** B3
Denby Grange CM17 . . .**35** A4
Denny Ct CM23 . . . . **5** A2
Devoils La **9** CM23. . . . .**11** B1
Deynes Rd CB11 . . . .**41** B3
Dimsdale Cres CM23 . . .**14** A2
Doctor's La CO10 . . . .**28** C2
Doddenhill Cl CB10 . . . .**31** A1
Dolphin Way CM23 . . . . .**11** C2
Dorset Ho **13** CM23. . . . .**11** B1
Doulton Cl CM17 . . . .**35** A3
Dove Cl
Bishop's Stortford
CM23 . . . .**13** A1
Stansted Mountfitchet
CM24 . . . . **4** B4
Dovehouse Croft CM20 .**27** C2
Downs Prim Sch The
CM20. . . . .**33** A4
Downs The CM20 . . . . . .**33** A4
Dragon's Gn CB10. . . . . .**36** C1
Drakes Mdw CM17 . . . . .**29** A4
Drayman's Cl CM23 . . . .**12** A3
Drive The
Harlow CM20. . . . .**27** A1
Sawbridgeworth CM21 . . .**19** A2
Drovers Way CM23 . . . . .**12** B3
Drummonds The CM16 .**38** C1
Duchess Cl CM23. . . . . . .**10** B1
DUCK END **6** A1
Ducketts Mead CM19 . . .**24** A3
Ducketts Wharf **10**
CM23 . . . .**13** B4

Duckling La CM21. . . . . .**19** A2
Duffs Hill CO10 . . . . **2** A1
Dukes Cl CM16. . . . .**43** A1
Dukes Ride CM23 . . . . . .**10** B1
Dunmow Rd
Bishop's Stortford
CM23 . . . .**14** B3
Takeley CM22 . . . .**17** A3
Dunstalls CM19 . . . .**31** C2
Durham Cl CM21 . . . .**18** B1
Dyers Ct CM23 . . . .**12** B3

E

Earls Cl CM23. . . . .**12** C4
East Dr CM21 . . . .**19** A1
EASTEND. **25** A3
Eastend Cotts CM19 . . . .**24** C3
East Gate CM20 . . . .**26** C1
East Pk
Harlow CM17. . . . .**28** B3
Sawbridgeworth CM21 . . .**19** A1
East Rd
Bishop's Stortford
CM23 . . . .**14** A3
Harlow CM20. . . . .**28** A4
East View CM22 . . . .**17** A4
Eastwick Rd CM20 . . . . .**26** A4
East Wlk CM20. . . . .**26** C1
Eaton Ho **5** CM23. . . . . .**14** A4
Edens Cl CM23 . . . .**14** A3
Edens Mount CM21. . . . .**19** B4
Edinburgh Gate CM20 . .**26** C3
Edinburgh Gdns CM23. .**13** A4
Edinburgh Pl CM20. . . . .**27** C4
Edinburgh Way CM20. . .**27** A3
Edmunds Ho CM16 . . . . .**40** C4
Edmund's Twr CM19 . . .**32** B4
Edward Ho CB10 . . . .**31** A1
Egg Hall CM16 . . . .**38** C2
Eider Ct CM23 . . . .**13** C4
Elderfield CM17. . . . .**28** C3
Eleventh Ave CM24. . . . . . **7** A2
Elizabeth Rd CM23 . . . . .**13** A3
Elizabeth Way CM20. . . .**26** A2
Ellenborough Cl CM23. .**12** C3
Elliott Ct CM23. . . . .**11** C2
Elmbridge CM17 . . . .**29** B3
Elmbrook Dr CM23 . . . . .**13** A1
Elm Cl
Elsenham CM22. . . . . **3** B3
Takeley CM22 . . . .**17** A3
Elm Close Extension
CM22. . . . .**17** A3
Elm Gdns CM16 . . . .**43** A2
Elm Gr CM23 . . . .**14** A3
Elm Rd CM23 . . . .**11** B2
Elms The CM5. . . . .**45** B2
Elmwood CM21 . . . .**19** B1
ELSENHAM **3** B2
Elsenham CE Prim Sch
CM22. . . . . **3** C2
Elsenham Cross CM22 . . **3** C2
Elsenham Sta CM22 . . . . **3** B4

Elwood CM17 . . . .**35** A4
Emberson Way CM16. . .**43** B2
Emmerson Ho CM23. . . .**13** C3
EPPING. **38** B2
Epping Inf Sch CM16 . . .**38** B1
Epping Jun Sch CM16 . .**38** B1
Epping Ongar Rly*
CM16 . . . .**43** C1
Epping Rd
Coopersale CM16 . . . . . .**39** C4
Roydon CM19 . . . .**30** C3
Epping Sta CM16. . . . . . .**41** A4
Everest Gdns CM23. . . . .**13** A4

F

Fairbank Cl CM5 . . . .**45** A3
Faircroft CM17. . . . .**28** B4
Fairfield Rd
Chipping Ongar CM5 . . . . .**45** A3
Epping CM16 . . . .**39** A2
Fairlawns CM16. . . . .**39** A2
Fair Leas CB10 . . . .**31** A1
Fairway
Bishop's Stortford
CM23 . . . .**14** B2
Sawbridgeworth CM21 . . .**19** B2
Fairway The CM18. . . . . .**33** C2
Falcon Cl CM21 . . . .**18** B1
Falconers Pk CM21. . . . . .**18** C1
Falconer St CM23 . . . . . .**12** B3
Fallowden La CB10. . . . .**33** B4
Farm Cl CM19. . . . .**24** A3
Farnham Cl CM21 . . . . . .**18** B1
Farriers CM21 . . . .**19** A3
Fawbert & Barnards Prim
Sch CM17. . . . .**28** B3
Fawbert & Bernard Inf Sch
CM21. . . . .**19** A2
Felmongers CM20. . . . . .**28** A2
Fenman Ct CM22. . . . . **3** B2
Fennells CM19 . . . .**36** B3
Fenner Brockway Ho
CM20. . . . .**33** A4
Fenton Grange CM17 . . .**34** B3
Fern Hill CO10 . . . . **2** A2
Fern Hill La CM18 . . . . . .**37** B3
Feryngs Cl CM17 . . . .**28** C4
Fesants Croft CM20 . . . .**28** A3
FIDDLERS HAMLET. **41** C3
Fifth Ave CM24. . . . . **7** A2
Fifth Ave / Allende Ave
CM20. . . . .**26** B3
Finch Ct CM5 . . . .**44** B2
Finchmoor CM18. . . . . . .**32** C1
Firlands CM23 . . . .**13** A4
Firlands Ho CM23 . . . . . .**13** A4
Fir Pk CM19 . . . .**32** A1
First Ave CM24. . . . . **7** A2
First Ave / Mandela Ave
CM20. . . . .**27** B2
Fir Trees CM16 . . . .**39** A2

Fishers Hatch CM20 . . . . 27 A1
Fitzwilliams Ct CM17 . . . 29 A4
Five Acres
  Harlow CM18 . . . . 33 A1
  Stansted Mountfitchet
  CM24 . . . . 4 B4
Flax La CO10 . . . . 20 A4
Flex Mdw CM19 . . . . 25 B1
Florence Cl CM17 . . . . . . 34 B2
Florence Wlk **8** CM23 . . 11 B2
Flux's La CM16 . . . . 41 A2
Fold Croft CM20 . . . . 25 C3
Fordwater Cl CO9 . . . . . . 26 A3
Forebury Ave CM21 . . . . 19 B2
Forebury Cres CM21. . . . 19 B2
Forebury The CM21. . . . . 19 B2
Forelands Pl CM21 . . . . . 19 A2
Fore St CM17 . . . . 28 B4
Forest Glade CM16 . . . . . 42 A1
Foresthall Rd CM24 . . . . . 6 A4
Forest Side CM16 . . . . . . 40 A2
Forge Cotts CM22 . . . . . . 21 A4
Fortunes The CM18. . . . . 33 B2
Foster St CM17 . . . . 35 C3
FOSTER STREET 35 B3
Fountain Farm CM18 . . 33 B2
Four Acres The CM21. . . 19 C2
Four Ash Hill CO9 . . . . . . 27 A1
Fourth Ave
  Harlow CM19 . . . . 32 A4
  Stansted Mountfitchet
  CM24 . . . . 7 A2
Four Wantz The CM5 . . . 44 B1
Fourways CM22 . . . . 3 B2
Foxdells La CM23 . . . . . . 11 B4
Foxes La CO10 . . . . 28 C1
Foxes Rd CO10 . . . . 29 A1
Foxglove Cl CM23 . . . . . . 12 B4
Foxley Dr CM23 . . . . 14 A4
Frampton Rd CM16. . . . . 38 C3
Francis Ct CM20 . . . . 26 A2
Frank Bretton Ho CM5. . 45 B4
Frere Ct CM23 . . . . 11 B3
Freshwaters CM20 . . . . . 27 A1
Friars The CM19. . . . . . . 31 C4
Friars Wood CM23 . . . . . 14 B4
Friedberg Ave CM23 . . . . 12 C2
Frogge St CB10 . . . . 21 C4
Fuller Ct **3** CM23 . . . . . . 11 C1
Fuller's Almshouses
  CM24 . . . . 4 C2
FULLER'S END 3 C1
Fullers Mead CM17. . . . . 34 B3
Fulton Cres CM23 . . . . . 14 B4
Furriers Cl CM23 . . . . . . 12 B3
Fyfield Bsns & Research
  Pk CM5 . . . . 44 C3
Fyfield Rd CM5 . . . . 44 B2

Gables The
  Chipping Ongar CM5 . . . . . 44 B2
  Sawbridgeworth CM21 . . . 19 A2
Gall End La CM24 . . . . 4 C3
Galloway Cl **1** CM23 . . . 11 B2
Galloway Rd CM23 . . . . . 11 B3
Garden Terrace Rd **2**
  CM17 . . . . 28 B4
Gardiners The CM17 . . . . 34 A4
Garnetts CM22 . . . . 16 C4
Garnon Mead CM16 . . . . 39 C3
GASTON GREEN 2 A2
Gatwick Cl CM23 . . . . 5 A1
Genevyll Cl CO10 . . . . . . 18 C2
George Avey Croft
  CM16 . . . . 43 A2
George Green Bglws
  CM22 . . . . 2 A4
George Green Villas
  CM22 . . . . 2 A3
Gerard Ave CM23. . . . . . . 13 A2
Gibb Croft CM18 . . . . 37 B4
Gibbs Field CM23 . . . . . . 12 C3
Gibson Cl CM16 . . . . 43 B3
Gibson Ct CM18 . . . . 33 A1
Gilbey Ave CM23 . . . . 14 A2
Gilbey Cotts CM22 . . . . . . 3 B2
Gilbey Cres CM24 . . . . 4 B4
Gilden Cl CM17 . . . . 29 A4
Gilden Way CM17 . . . . . . 28 C3
Gilders CM21 . . . . 18 C2
Gipsy La CM23, CM24. . . . . 5 B4
Gladden Ct CM18. . . . . . . 37 A4
Glan Avon Mews CM17 . 34 B3
Glebe Ct CM23 . . . . 14 A4
Glebe End CM20 . . . . 3 C2
Glebelands CM20 . . . . . . 27 B3
Glebe Rd CM5 . . . . 45 A3
Glebe The
  Elsenham CM22. . . . . 3 B2
  Harlow CM20. . . . . 27 A1
Goddard Way CB10. . . . . 31 A1
Godsafe CM17 . . . . 29 A4
Gold Cl CM22 . . . . 3 A4
Goldings CM23. . . . . 14 A4
Golds Nursery Bsns Pk
  CM22 . . . . 3 B4
Goodliffe Pk CM23 . . . . . 5 A2
Goodwin Stile CM23. . . . 12 C3
Gorefield CM22 . . . . 17 A3
Gorefield Rdbt CM24 . . . 9 A4
Gowers The CM20 . . . . . . 28 A2
Grace Gdns CM23 . . . . . . 13 B2
Grailands CM23 . . . . 10 C2
Granary Ct CM21 . . . . 19 A2
Granary The CM19. . . . . . 24 A3
Grange La CM19 . . . . 24 B2
Grange Pk CM23 . . . . 11 B3
Grange Rd CM23 . . . . 11 C1
Grangeside CM23 . . . . . . 11 C4
Grange The CM23 . . . . . . 11 B3
Grange Wlk CM23 . . . . . . 11 C1

Granville Rd CM16 . . . . . 39 A2
Gravel Pit Farm CM19 . . 32 B2
Grays Ct CM23 . . . . 11 A2
Great Augur St **4**
  CM17 . . . . 28 C1
Great Brays CM18 . . . . . . 33 C3
Great Eastern Cl CM23. . 13 C4
Great Gregories La
  CM16 . . . . 40 B2
Great Hadham Rd
  CM23 . . . . 12 B3
Great Havers Ct CM23 . . 13 A3
Great Lawn CM5 . . . . 44 B1
Great Leylands CM18 . . . 33 C3
GREAT PARNDON 32 A2
Great Plumtree CM20 . . 27 B2
GREAT SAMPFORD 43 A1
Great Stony Pk CM5 . . . . 44 B1
Greenacres CM16 . . . . . . 38 B3
Greenfields CM24 . . . . . . 4 B3
Greenhill Pk CM23 . . . . . 12 C3
Greenhills CM20 . . . . 33 A4
Green La CM17. . . . . 35 C2
Green Pk CM20 . . . . 33 A4
Green St **2** CM17 . . . . . 28 C1
Greenstead CM21 . . . . . . 19 A1
Greenstead Rd CM5 . . . . 45 A3
Green The
  Bishop's Stortford
  CM23 . . . . 13 B2
  Saffron Walden CB10 . . . . 30 C1
Green Trees CM16 . . . . . . 41 A4
Greenway
  Bishop's Stortford
  CM23 . . . . 14 B2
  Harlow CM19. . . . . 25 A2
Greenway Bsns Ctr
  CM19 . . . . 25 A2
Green Wlk CM5 . . . . 45 B2
Greygoose Pk CM19 . . . . 31 C3
Greys Cl CO10. . . . . 18 B1
Griffin's Wood Cotts
  CM16 . . . . 40 A3
Grinstead La CM22 . . . . . . 2 B1
Grosvenor Cl CM23. . . . . 12 C2
Grosvenor Ho **4** CM23 . 14 A4
Grove Hill CM24. . . . . 4 C3
Grove La CM16. . . . . 38 C1
Grove Pk CM23 . . . . 10 B2
Grove Pl **19** CM23 . . . . . 11 B1
Guildhall Way CB10 . . . 33 C3
Guilfords CM17 . . . . 23 A1

Hadham Ct CM23. . . . . . . 11 A2
Hadham Gr CM23 . . . . . . 10 B2
Hadham Rd CM23 . . . . . . 10 C2
Hadley Grange CM17 . . 34 B3
Hailes Wood CM22 . . . . . 3 C2
Hailes Wood Cl CM22. . . 3 C2
Half Acres CM23 . . . . 11 B2
Half Moon Cotts CM21. . 18 A1
Half Moon La CM16 . . . . 40 C4

Hall Barns CM24 . . . . 4 A3
Hallingbury Cl CM22 . . . . 2 A4
Hallingbury Rd CM21. . . 19 C4
Halling Hill CM20 . . . . . . 27 B2
Hall Rd CM22 . . . . 3 C2
HALLS GREEN. 30 B3
Hamlet Hill CM19 . . . . . . 30 A2
Hammarskjold Rd
  CM20 . . . . 26 C2
Hampden Cl CM16 . . . . . 42 C1
Hampton Gdns CM21. . . 22 C3
Hamstel Rd CM20 . . . . . . 26 B1
Hand La CM21 . . . . 18 B1
Hanover Ct CM21 . . . . . . 19 B1
Hansells Mead CM19 . . . 24 A3
Harberts Rd CM19. . . . . . 32 A4
Harding Ho CM16 . . . . . . 41 A4
Harefield CM20 . . . . 27 C1
Hare St CM19 . . . . 32 A4
HARE STREET. 32 A3
Hare Street Com Prim Sch
  CM19 . . . . 32 B4
Hare Street Springs
  CM19 . . . . 32 A4
Hargrave Cl CM24. . . . . . . 4 B4
HARLOW 28 B2
Harlow Bsns Pk CM19 . . 25 A2
Harlowbury Prim Sch
  CM17 . . . . 28 C4
Harlow Coll CM20 . . . . . . 26 C1
Harlow Comm CM17. . . . 34 C2
Harlow Fields Sch
  CM18 . . . . 33 A2
Harlow Mill Sta CM20 . . 22 C1
Harlow Rd
  Roydon CM19 . . . . 24 B3
  Sawbridgeworth CM21 . . . 22 C4
Harlow Ret Pk CM20 . . . 27 B4
Harlow Seedbed Ctr
  CM19 . . . . 25 C1
Harlow Stad (Greyhounds)
  CM19 . . . . 25 A3
Harlow Town Sta CM20 . 26 C3
Harold Cl CM19 . . . . 25 B1
Harolds Rd CM19. . . . . . . 25 B1
Harp La CO10 . . . . 20 A1
Harrington Cl **7** CM23 . 11 C1
Harrison Dr CM16 . . . . . . 43 A2
Harrisons CM23. . . . . 5 C2
Harrowband Rd **7**
  CM17 . . . . 28 B1
Hartland Rd CM16. . . . . . 38 C1
Hart Rd CM17 . . . . 22 C2
Harvest Fields CM22 . . . 16 C3
Harvey Ctr CM20 . . . . . . 32 C4
Haslemere CM23. . . . . . . 13 C2
Haslemere Ind Est
  CM23 . . . . 13 C2
Haslemere Pinnacles Est
  The CM19. . . . . 25 C1
Hastingswood Bsns Ctr
  CM17 . . . . 35 C1
Hastingwood Ct CM5. . . 44 B2
Hatch Gn CM22 . . . . 2 A3

Hatfield Heath......21 C4
Hatfield Heath Com Prim
 Sch CM22.............21 B4
Havers La CM23........13 B3
Havers Par CM23.......13 B3
Hawkenbury CM19 .....32 A2
Hawks Hill CM16.......42 C1
Hawthorn Cl CM22 .....17 A3
Hawthorn Rise CM23 ..13 B1
Hawthorns CM18.......37 B4
Haycroft CM23.........14 B3
Haydens Rd CM20......32 B4
Hayley Bell Gdns CM23 .13 B1
Haymeads La CM23 ....14 B2
Hazelend Rd CM23 ......5 A4
Hazel Gdns CM21 ......19 B1
Heathcote Gdns CM17. .35 A4
Heather Cl CM23.......12 C4
Heath Row CM23........5 A1
Hedgerows CM21 ......19 B2
Hedgerows The CM23 ..14 A2
Heighams CM19 ....31 B3
Helions Rd CM19.......32 A4
Hemnal Ho CM16 ......40 B3
Hemnall St CM16.......40 C4
Hemnal Mews CM16...38 C1
Henry Moore Prim Sch
 The CM17.............34 C3
Herald Cl CM23........12 C4
Hermitage Ct CM24 .....4 A3
Hermitage Ho CM24.....4 A3
Heron Cl CM21.........18 C1
Heron Ct
 Bishop's Stortford
 CM23................11 C1
 Chipping Ongar CM5 .....44 B2
Herons Wood CM20 ....26 A2
Hertfordshire & Essex
 High Sch The CM23...14 A3
Herts & Essex Com Hospl
 CM23................14 A2
Hester Ho CM20.......26 B2
Hides The CM20.......26 C1
Higham View CM16.....43 B4
High Elms CM18 ....33 B2
Highfield
 Harlow CM18..........33 C3
 Sawbridgeworth CM21 ..19 A3
Highfield Ave CM23 ....14 B2
Highfield Gn CM16 ....40 B4
Highfield Pl CM16......40 B4
Highfields CB11.......41 B3
Highgate Gr CM21.....18 C2
High House Est CM17. .29 B4
High La CM24..........4 C4
Highland Rd CM23 .....13 B1
Highmead CM24 ....4 B4
High Ongar Rd
 (Chelmsford Rd) CM5. .44 C2
High Pastures CM22....20 B1
High Rd
 Epping CM16...........40 A3
 North Weald Bassett
 CM16................43 A2

High St
 Bishop's Stortford
 CM23................11 B1
 Cavendish CO10 ....18 C2
 Chipping Ongar CM5.....45 B4
 Debden CB11..........41 B3
 Elsenham CM22.........3 C2
 Epping CM16...........40 C4
 Harlow CM17...........28 B4
 Roydon CM19 ....24 A3
High View CM23.........5 C3
HIGH WYCH 18 A1
High Wych Rd CM21.....18 A1
Hillcrest Way CM16.....41 A4
Hillmead Prim Sch
 CM23................10 B1
Hillside CM17.........34 B2
Hillside Ave CM23......11 C1
Hillside Cotts CM23 .....5 B3
Hillside End CM23.......5 B3
Hill Terr CO10..........20 A1
Hill The CM17.........28 B4
Hill Tree Cl CM21......18 C1
Hilly Field CM18 ....37 B4
Hintons CM19.........31 C2
Hipkins CM23.........13 A2
HOBBS CROSS 29 C1
Hobbs Cross Rd CM17 .29 B3
Hobbs La CO10.........20 B3
Hobtoe Rd CM20.......25 C3
HOCKERILL 13 C4
Hockerill Anglo-European
 Coll CM23............14 A3
Hockerill Ct 6 CM23 ...11 C1
Hockerill St CM23......11 C1
Hodings Rd CM20......26 B2
Hoestock Rd CM21.....18 C2
Holland Way CM17.....28 C1
Hollow Rd CO10.......29 A3
Holly Cotts CM16......40 A3
Hollyfield CM19.......32 B1
Holmes Mdw CM19.....36 A2
Holy Cross RC Prim Sch
 CM18................33 C2
Home Cl CM20.........33 B4
Homefield Cl CM16....38 C1
Home Mead CM18......32 C2
Honeybourne CM23 ....13 A2
Honeymeade CM21.....22 C3
Honeysuckle Cl CM23 .12 B4
Honor St 7 CM17......28 C1
Hook Field CM18.......33 B2
Hoo The CM17.........22 C1
HOPE END GREEN......17 C1
Hornbeams The CM20 .26 B2
Horsecroft Pl CM19 ....25 A1
Horsecroft Rd CM19....25 A1
Horshams CM19 ....32 B4
Houblons Hill
 Coopersale CM16.......39 C1
 Epping CM16...........41 C4
House on the Hill Toy Mus
 The* CM24 ....4 C3
Howard Way CM20 .....27 B2

Howe La CB10 ....42 C2
HOWE STREET 45 A2
Hows Mead CM16 ......43 C4
Hugh's Twr 4 CM20....26 C1
Hugh Villas CM23.......13 C3
Hull Gr CM19 ....31 C1
Hunters Chase CM5 ....45 B2
Hunters Ct CM22 ....3 B3
Hurn Gr CM23..........5 B1
Hurricane Way CM16...42 C1
Hurst Cl CM23 ....11 A1
Hyde Park Cnr CO10....18 C2

I

Icknield Cl CB10 ....21 B4
Inchcape CM16.........41 A2
Ingels Mead CM16 .....38 B2
Institute Rd CM16......39 C2
Integrated Support Ctr,
 PRU CM18.............37 B4
Irving Cl CM23 ....12 C2
Island Ct CM23........13 C3
Italstyle Bldg The
 CM20................22 C2
IVY CHIMNEYS........40 B3
Ivy Chimneys CM16....40 B3
Ivy Chimneys Prim Sch
 CM16................40 C3
Ivy Chimneys Rd CM16. .40 B3
Ivy Todd Hill CB11......41 A4

J

Jack's La CM22 ....17 B3
Jacksons Cl CM5.......45 B3
Jackson Sq 10 CM23 ...11 B1
Jack Stevens Cl CM17 .34 B2
James St CM16 ....38 C3
Jasmin Cl CM23........12 B4
J Ct CM20 ....27 B1
Jeans La CM23........11 A1
Jenkins Dr CM22.......3 B4
Jenkins La CM22......14 B1
Jerounds CM19 ....32 A2
Jerounds Com Jun & Inf
 Sch CM19.............32 A1
Jervis Rd CM23 ....13 B4
Jim Desormeaux Bglws
 CM20................27 A2
Jocelyns CM17........28 B4
John Dyde Cl CM23 ....13 C4
Johns Rd CM23 ....11 C3
Johns The CM5 ....44 B1
Joscelyn's Yd 11 CM23. .11 C1
Joyners Field CM18 ....36 B4
Jubilee Cott 12 CM23...11 C1

K

Kate's La CB10.........34 B4
KATHERINES...........31 B3
Katherines Hatch
 CM19................31 C4

Katherines Ho CM19 . . .31 C4
Katherines Prim Sch
 CM19................31 C4
Katherine's Way CM19. .31 C4
Kebbles CO10..........2 A1
Kecksy's CM21........19 B4
Keefield CM19 ....36 A3
Kendal Ave CM16......41 A4
Kent Cres CM23.......13 A2
Kerril Croft CM20 ......25 C3
Kestrel Gdns CM23 ....12 B4
Kettlebury Way CM5...45 A2
Kilnfield CM5 ....45 A3
Kiln La CM17..........34 B3
Kiln Rd CM16 ....42 C1
Kimberley Cl CM23 ....13 C3
Kimpton's Cl CM5......44 A2
Kingfisher Way CM23...11 C1
Kingsbridge Rd CM23 .11 C2
King's Cotts CM23......13 C4
Kings Ct CM23 ....11 C2
Kingsdon La CM17.....34 B3
Kings Head Ct CM21....19 A2
Kingsland CM18.......32 B2
Kingsmead CM21......19 A1
Kingsmead Cl CM19....24 A1
Kingsmead Hill CM19...24 A1
Kingsmead Rd CM23 ..11 C2
Kings Mews CM21......19 A2
KINGSMOOR...........36 B3
Kingsmoor Prim Sch
 CM18................36 B4
Kingsmoor Rd CM19...32 A1
King St CM23 ....11 B1
King Street Mews 1
 CM23................11 B1
Kitson Way CM20......26 B1
Knebworth Ct CM23 ...12 C4
Knights Cl CM23 ......10 B2
Knight's Ct CM21......19 A2
Knights Row CM23 ....13 A4
Knight St CM21 ....19 A2

L

Laburnum Cl CM22.....20 A1
Laburnum Rd CM16 ...39 B2
Ladyshot CM20 ....28 A1
Ladywell Prospect
 CM21................19 C1
Lambert Cross CB10....31 A1
Lancaster Rd CM16.....42 C2
Lancaster Way CM23 ..10 B2
Landview Gdns CM5....45 B2
Lane End CM17 ....35 A3
Larchwood CM23 .....12 C3
Larkspur Cl CM23 .....12 C4
Larksway CM23 ....12 B4
Larkswood CM17......34 B2
Latchmore Bank CM22 . .2 A3
LATTON BUSH.........34 A1

Latton Bush Bsns Ctr The
CM18 . . . . 33 B1
Latton Common Rd
CM18 . . . . 34 A1
Latton Gn CM18 . . . . 37 B4
Latton Green Prim Sch
CM18 . . . . 37 B4
Latton Hall Cl CM20 . . . . 27 C1
Latton Ho CM18 . . . . 34 A1
Latton St
Harlow, Brays Grove CM18,
CM20 . . . . 34 A3
Harlow, Potter Street
CM17 . . . . 34 B1
Lavender Cl
Bishop's Stortford
CM23 . . . . 12 C4
Harlow CM20 . . . . 27 A1
Lawn The CM20 . . . . 28 A3
Lawrence Ave CM21 . . . 19 A4
Lawrence Moorings
CM21 . . . . 19 B2
Lea Cl CM23 . . . . 5 A1
Lea Gr CM23 . . . . 5 A1
Lea Hall Bglws CM22 . . 21 C4
Leat Cl CM21 . . . . 19 B3
Legions Way CM23 . . . . . 11 C2
Leigh Dr CM22 . . . . 3 B2
Leonard Davis Ho
CM16 . . . . 42 C1
Leventhorpe Sch The
CM21 . . . . 19 A4
Ley Field CM22 . . . . 17 A3
Limefields CB10 . . . . 30 C2
Limes Cres CM23 . . . . . . 11 C1
Lincoln Cl CM23 . . . . 12 C3
Lincolns Field CM16 . . . 38 B1
Lindens The CM23 . . . . . 13 B4
Lindsey Cl CM23 . . . . 11 B3
Lindsey Rd CM23 . . . . . . 11 B3
Lindsey St CM16 . . . . 38 C2
Linford Cl CM19 . . . . 32 B2
Linford End CM19 . . . . . 32 B2
Link Rd CM23 . . . . 11 B2
Links Bsns Ctr The
CM23 . . . . 14 B3
Linkside Rd CM23 . . . . . . 14 B2
Link Way CM23 . . . . 13 A4
Linwood CM21 . . . . 19 A2
Little Brays CM18 . . . . . 33 C2
Little Brook Rd CM19 . . 24 B2
Little Cattins CM19 . . . . 31 B2
Little Gregories La
CM16 . . . . 40 A1
Little Grove Field CM19 32 B4
LITTLE HALLINGBURY . . 2 B3
Little Hallingbury CE Prim
Sch CM22 . . . . 2 B4
Little Heath CM22 . . . . . 21 B4
LITTLE PARNDON 26 A1
Little Parndon Sch
CM20 . . . . 26 A1

Little Pynchons CM18 . . 33 C1
LITTLE WALDEN 25 B2
Little Walden Rd CB10 . . 31 A3
Little Wlk CM20 . . . . 32 C4
Livingstone Cl CM5 . . . . 45 B3
Livingstone Cotts CM5 . 45 B3
Loates Pasture CM24 . . . . 4 A4
Lock View CM21 . . . . 19 B2
Lodge Farm Rd CO10 . . . 20 A4
Lodge Hall CM18 . . . . . . 37 A4
Lodge The CM16 . . . . 38 C1
London Rd
Bishop's Stortford
CM23 . . . . 13 C3
Harlow CM17 . . . . 28 B2
Sawbridgeworth CM21 . . 19 A2
London Stansted Airport
CM24 . . . . 8 B3
Long Acre CM17 . . . . 28 A4
Long Banks CM18 . . . . . . 32 C1
Long Border Rd CM24 . . 8 A1
Longcroft CM22 . . . . 17 A3
Long Croft CM24 . . . . 4 A4
Longfield CM18 . . . . 33 C2
Long Fields CM5 . . . . 45 B2
Long Ho CM18 . . . . 33 B2
Longland Bridge CM22 . 20 A1
Long Ley CM20 . . . . 33 B4
Long Meadow CM23 . . . 12 C4
Long Pastures CO10 . . . . 20 A4
Long Wood CM18 . . . . . . 36 C3
Loppys Hill **1** CM24 . . . . . 4 B2
Lords Ave CM23 . . . . 10 A1
Lords Cl CB10 . . . . 36 C1
Love La CM5 . . . . 45 B4
Lovet Rd CM19 . . . . 25 C1
Lower Bury La CM16 . . . 40 B4
Lower Gn CO10 . . . . 28 B4
LOWER GREEN 38 A2
Lower Mdw CM18 . . . . . 37 A4
Lower Park Cres CM23 . 13 B3
Lower Rd CM22 . . . . 2 B2
Lower Sheering CM21 . . 19 C3
Lower St
Cavendish CO10 . . . . 18 C1
Stansted Mountfitchet
CM24 . . . . 4 C3
Lower Swaines CM16 . . . 38 B1
Lowfield CM21 . . . . 19 A1
Low St CO10 . . . . 2 B1
Luxford Pl CM21 . . . . 19 B1
Lynceley Grange CM16 . 38 C2
Lynton Ct CM23 . . . . 13 A2
Lysander Ct CM16 . . . . . 43 A2

M

Mabey's Wlk CM21 . . . . . 18 A1
Maddox Rd CM20 . . . . . . 33 A4
Madeleines Flats CM19 . 32 A3
Madells CM16 . . . . 40 C4
Magnaville Rd CM23 . . . 13 A2
Maitland Rd CM24 . . . . . . 4 B2
Malkin Dr CM17 . . . . 35 A3

Mallard Ct CM23 . . . . 13 C4
Mallards Rise CM17 . . . . 34 C4
Mallories CM20 . . . . 27 B2
Mallows Gn CM19 . . . . . 31 C1
Maltings Dr CM16 . . . . . 38 C2
Maltings La CM16 . . . . . . 38 C2
Maltings The CO10 . . . . . 18 C2
Mandeville Cl CM17 . . . 34 B2
Mandeville Prim Sch
CM21 . . . . 18 C3
Manor Cl CO10 . . . . 18 B2
Manor Fields Prim Sch
CM23 . . . . 12 C3
Manor Hatch CM18 . . . . 33 C3
Manor Hatch Cl CM18 . . 34 A3
Manor Links CM23 . . . . . 14 B3
Manor Rd
Bishop's Stortford
CM23 . . . . 11 C1
Harlow CM17 . . . . 22 C1
Stansted Mountfitchet
CM24 . . . . 4 B1
Manston Dr CM23 . . . . . . 5 A1
Manston Rd CM20 . . . . . 33 A4
Maple Ave CM23 . . . . 10 C2
Maple Cl CM23 . . . . 10 C2
Maple Gr CM23 . . . . 10 C2
Maple River Ind Est
CM20 . . . . 22 B2
Maple Spring CM23 . . . . 10 C2
Maples The CM19 . . . . . . 36 A3
MARDEN ASH 45 B2
Mardyke Rd CM20 . . . . . 27 C2
Margaret Cl CM16 . . . . . 38 B2
Margaret Rd CM16 . . . . . 38 C2
Margrave Gdns **4**
CM23 . . . . 13 A3
Marguerite Way CM23 . 12 B4
Marigold Pl CM17 . . . . . 28 A4
Market Ho **2** CM20 . . . 26 C1
Market Sq **6** CM23 . . . 11 B1
Market St
7 Bishop's Stortford
CM23 . . . . 11 B1
Harlow CM17 . . . . 28 B4
Mark Hall Cycle Mus &
Gdns* CM20 . . . . 28 A3
Mark Hall Moors CM20 . 28 A3
MARK HALL NORTH . . . 27 C3
Mark Hall Sch CM17 . . . 28 B3
MARK HALL SOUTH . . . 27 C1
Mark's Ave CM5 . . . . 44 B1
Markwells CM22 . . . . 3 C3
Markwell Wood CM19 . . 36 A2
Marlands CM21 . . . . 19 A4
Marlborough Cl CM23 . . 13 B3
Marquis Cl CM23 . . . . . . 10 A1
Marriotts CM17 . . . . 22 C1
Marshbarns CM23 . . . . . 10 B2
Marshgate Ctr CM19 . . . 24 C2
Marsh La CM17 . . . . 23 B1
Mary McArthur Pl CM24 . 4 B4
Mary Park Gdns CM23 . . 13 B2

Masons Ct
Bishop's Stortford
CM23 . . . . 11 A1
Stansted Mountfitchet
CM24 . . . . 4 A2
Masterman Wharf **12**
CM23 . . . . 11 B1
Matching La CM23 . . . . . 10 C2
Matching Rd
Harlow, Matching
CM22 . . . . 21 C1
Hatfield Heath CM22 . . . 21 C3
Mathams Dr CM23 . . . . . 12 C3
Mathews Villas CM19 . . 31 A4
Maunds Farm CM18 . . . 37 A4
Maunds Hatch CM18 . . . 37 A4
Mayes Cl CM23 . . . . 14 C4
Mayfield Cl CM17 . . . . . . 29 B4
Mayfield Pk CM23 . . . . . 12 C1
Mayflower Ct
Chipping Ongar CM5 . . . 44 B1
Harlow CM19 . . . . 36 A4
Mayflower Gdns CM23 . 12 C4
Mayflower Way CM5 . . . 44 B1
Maylins Dr CM21 . . . . . . 18 C2
Maypole St CM17 . . . . . . 28 B1
Maytree Gdns CM22 . . . . 3 A4
Maze Green Hts CM23 . . 10 B1
Maze Green Rd CM23 . . 10 C1
Mazoe Cl CM23 . . . . 13 B3
Mazoe Rd CM23 . . . . 13 B3
Mead Ct CM24 . . . . 4 A3
Meadowcroft CM24 . . . . 4 B3
Meadow Ct CM18 . . . . . . 37 A4
Meadowlands CM23 . . . 11 C4
Meadow Rd CM16 . . . . . 38 C2
Meadows The
Bishop's Stortford
CM23 . . . . 13 A3
Sawbridgeworth CM21 . . 19 C2
Meadowsweet Cl CM23 12 B4
Meadow Way CM21 . . . . 19 C1
Mead Park Ind Est
CM20 . . . . 27 B4
Meads The CM24 . . . . 4 C2
Mead Wlk CM5 . . . . 45 A2
Melford Rd CO10 . . . . . . 19 A2
Mercers CM19 . . . . 31 C3
Mercers Ave CM23 . . . . . 12 B2
Merefield CM21 . . . . 19 A1
Merlin Way CM16 . . . . . . 42 C3
Merrill Pl **2** CM23 . . . . . 13 A3
Merring Way CM19 . . . . 25 B1
Mews The
Bishop's Stortford
CM22 . . . . 13 C1
Harlow CM18 . . . . 37 A4
Sawbridgeworth CM21 . . 19 A3
Stansted Mountfitchet
CM24 . . . . 4 C3
Mia Ct CM19 . . . . 32 A4
Michaels Rd CM23 . . . . . . 5 A2
Middle Row **5** CM23 . . . 13 B4

Middleside Cvn Pk
CM24 . . . . 6 C4
Miles Cl CM19 . . . . .32 A3
Millbank Ave CM5 . . . . .45 A3
Mill Cl CM22 . . . . 3 B2
Millcroft CM23 . . . . .11 C3
Mill Ct CM20 . . . . .26 C3
Millers Cl CM23 . . . . .12 B3
Millersdale CM19 . . . . . .36 A4
Mill Field CM17 . . . . . . .28 B4
Millfields
Sawbridgeworth CM21 . . .19 B3
Stansted Mountfitchet
CM24 . . . . 4 B2
Mill Hatch CM20 . . . . . . .27 C4
Mill Hill CM24 . . . . 4 B2
Millhurst Mews CM17 . .29 A4
Milliners Way CM23 . . . .12 B2
Mill La
Cavendish CO10 . . . . . . .21 C1
Finchingfield CM7 . . . . . .45 A4
Harlow CM17 . . . . .29 A4
Hatfield Heath CM22 . . . .21 A4
Sawbridgeworth CM21 . . .19 B3
Mill Rd
Birdbrook CO9 . . . . .27 A2
Debden CB11 . . . . .41 B4
Mill Side CM24 . . . . 4 B2
Millside Ind Est CM23 . .13 C3
Mill St
Bishop's Stortford
CM23 . . . . .13 C3
Harlow CM17 . . . . .35 B1
Milton Cres CM5 . . . . . .44 A2
Milwards CM19 . . . . . . .36 A4
Milwards Prim Sch
CM19 . . . . .36 A4
Minchen Rd CM20 . . . . . .27 C1
Minton La CM17 . . . . . . .34 B4
Mistley Rd CM20 . . . . . . .27 C2
Mitre Bldgs 🟥 CM20 . . .26 B1
Mitre Gdns CM23 . . . . . .13 C2
Moat Ho CM19 . . . . .25 A1
Momples Rd CM20 . . . . .28 A1
Monksbury CM18 . . . . . .33 C1
Monk's Cnr CB10 . . . . . . .43 A1
Monkswick Rd CM20 . . .27 B1
Monkswood Dr CM23 . . .12 C4
Moore Twr CM18 . . . . . . .33 B3
Moorfields CM18 . . . . . . .36 B4
Moor Hall La
Bishop's Stortford
CM23 . . . . .12 B1
Bishop's Stortford, Thorley
CM23 . . . . .12 A1
Moor Hall Rd CM17 . . . .29 C4
Moorings The CM23 . . . .13 C3
Moorlands Reach
CM21 . . . . .19 C1
Moreton Rd CM5 . . . . . . .44 A4
Morley Gr CM20 . . . . . . .26 B2
Morningtons CM19 . . . . .36 B4
Morris Harp CB10 . . . . . .31 A1
Morris Ho CM18 . . . . .32 B1

MOTT'S GREEN 2 C1
Mount Dr CM24 . . . . 4 B1
Mountfitchet Castle &
Norman Village★
CM24 . . . . .4 C2
Mountfitchet Mathematics
& Computing Coll The
CM24 . . . . 6 B4
Mountfitchet Rd CM24 . . 4 B1
Mowbray Rd CM20 . . . . .27 C3
Mulberry Ct CM23 . . . . . .13 C3
Mulberry Gn CM17 . . . . .28 C4
Mulberry Terr CM17 . . . .28 A4
Muskham Rd CM20 . . . . .28 A3
Myson Way CM23 . . . . . .14 A3

N

Nails La 🟥 CM23 . . . . . . .11 B1
Nails Lane Ho 🟥 CM23 . .11 B1
Nelson Rd CM23 . . . . . . .13 C3
Nether Rd CO10 . . . . .18 C2
NETTESWELL 27 B1
Netteswellbury Farm
CM18 . . . . .33 B3
Netteswell Cross CM20 .27 A2
Netteswell Orch CM20 . .26 C1
Netteswell Rd CM20 . . . .27 A3
Netteswell Rectory
CM20 . . . . .33 A4
Netteswell Twr 🟥
CM20 . . . . .26 C1
New Barn La CM22 . . . . . .2 C4
Newbury Cl CM23 . . . . . .11 A2
New Court Bsns Pk
CM18 . . . . .36 B4
New Frontiers Science Pk
CM19 . . . . .31 B4
New Horizon Bsns Ctr
CM19 . . . . .25 B2
New Path CM23 . . . . .13 B4
Newports CM21 . . . . .18 B1
New Rd
Elsenham CM22 . . . . 3 B3
Harlow CM17 . . . . .28 C4
New Row CM22 . . . . .20 A1
New St CM21 . . . . .19 A3
Newton Dr CM21 . . . . . . .18 C1
NEW TOWN 13 B4
Newtown Rd CM23 . . . . .13 B4
Nicholl Rd CM16 . . . . . . .40 C4
Nicholls Field CM18 . . . .34 A3
Nightingales CM23 . . . . .14 A3
Ninth Ave CM24 . . . . 7 A2
Nobles The CM23 . . . . . . .12 C4
Norfolk Way CM23 . . . . .13 B3
Norman Ave CM23 . . . . .12 C4
Norman Ct CM24 . . . . 4 B3
Norman's Way CM24 . . . 4 B3
Norris Cl CM23 . . . . .14 B3
Northbrooks CM19 . . . . .32 B3
Northfield Rd CM21 . . . .19 A4
Northfields CM24 . . . . 4 B3
North Gate CM20 . . . . . .26 B1

Northgate End CM23 . . .11 B2
Northgate Prim Sch
CM23 . . . . .11 A2
North Gr CM18 . . . . .33 C3
North Ho CM18 . . . . .33 B2
Northolt Ave CM23 . . . . .5 A1
North Pl CM20 . . . . .22 B1
North Rd CM22 . . . . .17 A4
North St 🟦 CM23 . . . . . .11 B1
North Terr 🟥 CM23 . . . . .11 B1
North Weald Airfield
Museum★ CB10 . . . . . . .42 C1
NORTH WEALD
BASSETT 43 B2
North Weald Sta★
CM16 . . . . .43 A1
Nursery Cl CM23 . . . . . . .13 B4
Nursery Fields CM21 . . .18 C2
Nursery Rd CM23 . . . . . .13 B4

O

Oak Dr CM21 . . . . .22 C4
Oak End CM18 . . . . .33 B2
Oak Glade CM16 . . . . . . .39 C2
Oak Hall CM23 . . . . .11 A2
Oaklands Cl CM23 . . . . . .5 A2
Oaklands Dr
Bishop's Stortford CM23 . . .5 A2
Harlow CM17 . . . . .34 B3
Oaklands Pk CM23 . . . . . 5 A2
Oakleigh Ct CM23 . . . . . .10 C2
Oakleigh Rise CM16 . . . .41 A3
Oak Piece CM16 . . . . . . .43 B3
Oak Rd CM16 . . . . .38 B1
Oaks Ret Pk CM20 . . . . . .27 B3
Oak St CM23 . . . . .13 B4
Oaktree Cl 🟦 CM23 . . . .11 B1
Oaktree Gdns CM17 . . . .34 C3
Oak View Cvn Pk CM24 . . 6 C4
Oakwood Est CM20 . . . .28 A4
OakWood Mews 🟥
CM17 . . . . .28 B4
Obrey Way CM23 . . . . . . .13 A1
Occasio Ho CM20 . . . . . .32 B4
Old Bell Cl CM24 . . . . 4 A2
Old Burylodge La CM24 . . 6 C4
Old Court Ho 🟥 CM24 . . 4 B2
Old Farm Yd CM22 . . . . .20 A1
Old Hall Rise CM17 . . . . .35 A4
OLD HARLOW 28 C4
Oldhouse Croft CM20 . . .27 A2
Old House La CM19 . . . . .31 A4
Oldhouse Villas CM22 . .17 A4
Old Maltings The 🟥
CM23 . . . . .11 C1
Old Mill La CM22 . . . . 2 A1
Old Orch CM18 . . . . .32 C2
Old Rd CM17 . . . . .23 A1
Old River La CM23 . . . . . .11 B1
Ongar Ent Ctr CM5 . . . . .44 B2
Ongar Sta★ CM5 . . . . . . .44 B1
Ongar War Meml Hospl
CM5 . . . . .44 B2

Onslow Gdns CM5 . . . . . .44 B1
Orchard Cl CM22 . . . . . . .20 A1
Orchard Croft CM20 . . . .27 C2
Orchard Lea CM21 . . . . . .18 B1
Orchard Rd CM23 . . . . . . .5 A1
Orchards The
Epping CM16 . . . . .41 A3
Sawbridgeworth CM21 . . .19 A3
Orchid Cl CM22 . . . . .16 C3
Oriole Way CM23 . . . . . . .12 B4
Osbourne Gdns 🟥
CM23 . . . . .13 A3
Ostler Cl CM23 . . . . .12 B2
Oxcroft CM23 . . . . .13 B1
Oxleys The CM17 . . . . . . .29 A4
Oziers CM22 . . . . 3 B3

P

Paddock Mead CM18 . . .36 B3
Paddocks The CO10 . . . .28 C1
Paddock The CM23 . . . . .12 C1
Pages Cl CM23 . . . . .12 C3
Paget Ct CM22 . . . . 3 B2
Palace Gdns CM23 . . . . . .13 A3
Palmers Hill CM16 . . . . .38 C2
Palmers La 🟥 CM23 . . . .11 B1
Pamela Gdns CM23 . . . . .13 B1
Pannells Ash CO10 . . . . .28 C1
Paringdon Jun Sch
CM18 . . . . .36 C4
Paringdon Rd CM18,
CM19 . . . . .36 B3
Park Ave
Bishop's Stortford
CM23 . . . . .13 B1
Harlow CM17 . . . . .34 B1
Park Cl CM16 . . . . .42 C1
Park Ct CM20 . . . . .26 C2
Park Dr CM22 . . . . .21 C3
Parkend CM19 . . . . .24 C2
Parkfields CM19 . . . . . . .24 A1
Park Hill CM17 . . . . .28 A4
Park La
Bishop's Stortford
CM23 . . . . .13 B2
Harlow CM20 . . . . .26 C2
Parklands CM16 . . . . .39 C2
Parkland Way CM5 . . . . .45 A2
Park Mead CM20 . . . . . . .26 A1
Park Rd
Elsenham CM22 . . . . 3 C2
Stansted Mountfitchet
CM24 . . . . 4 B2
Park Side CM16 . . . . .39 A2
Parkway
Harlow CM19 . . . . .25 A2
Sawbridgeworth CM21 . . .19 B1
Parnall Rd CM18 . . . . . . .36 C4
Parndon Mill La CM20 . .26 A3
Parndon Wood Nature
Reserve★ CM19 . . . . . . .36 C2

Parndon Wood Rd CM18,
CM19 . . . . **36** B3
Parsloe Rd CM19 . . . . **36** A3
Parsonage Farm La
CB10 . . . . **43** A1
Parsonage Farm Trad Est
CM24 . . . . **6** B3
Parsonage La
Bishop's Stortford
CM23 . . . . **14** B4
Stansted Mountfitchet
CM24 . . . . **6** B4
Parsonage Leys CM20 . . **33** B4
Parsonage Rd CM22 . . . . **17** A4
Partridge Ct CM18 . . . . . . **33** A2
Partridge Rd CM18 . . . . . **32** C1
PASSMORES **32** C2
Passmores Sch & Tech
Coll CM18 . . . . **32** C3
Pastures The CM22 . . . . . **16** C3
Patmore Cl CM23 . . . . . . **10** B2
Patricia Gdns CM23 . . . . **13** A3
Patticroft CO10 . . . . **2** A1
Pavilions The
Chipping Ongar CM5 . . . . . **44** B1
North Weald Bassett
CM16 . . . . **43** B3
Paycock Rd CM19 . . . . . . **31** C4
Peacocks CM19 . . . . **31** B4
Peacocks Cl CO10 . . . . . . **18** B2
Peacocks Rd CO10 . . . . . . **18** B2
Pear Tree Mead CM18 . . **33** C1
Pear Tree Mead Prim Sch
CM18 . . . . **33** C1
Peasleys Yd CM23 . . . . . . **14** A3
Pegrams Ct CM18 . . . . . . **32** B1
Pegrams Rd CM18 . . . . . . **32** B1
Peldon Rd CM19 . . . . . . **31** C4
Pelly Ct CM16 . . . . **40** C4
Penlow Rd CM18 . . . . **32** C1
Penningtons CM23 . . . . . . **12** B3
Pennymead CM20 . . . . . . **27** C1
Penshurst CM17 . . . . **28** B3
Pentlow Dr CO10 . . . . . . **19** A1
Pentlow La CO10 . . . . . . **19** A1
Peregrine Cl CM23 . . . . . **12** C4
Perry Rd CM18 . . . . **36** B4
Perry Spring CM17 . . . . . **34** C2
Peterswood CM18 . . . . . . **36** C4
Peterswood Inf Sch
CM18 . . . . **36** C4
Petlands CB10 . . . . **25** B2
Pewterers Ave CM23 . . . **12** B2
Phelips Rd CM19 . . . . **36** A3
Pig La CM22 . . . . **13** C1
Pigotts Way CM23 . . . . . . **13** A3
Pike Way CM16 . . . . **42** C1
Pilkingtons CM17 . . . . . . **34** C4
Pinceybrook Rd CM18 . . **36** B4
Pincey Rd CM24 . . . . **8** B3
Pincey Rdbt CM24 . . . . . . **8** C3
Pine Gr CM23 . . . . **14** A2

Pinelands CM23 . . . . **11** B3
Pines Hill CM24 . . . . **4** A1
Pine View Manor CM16 . **38** C1
Pinewood Cl CM17 . . . . . **34** B3
PINNACLES **25** C2
Pishiobury Dr CM21 . . . . **23** A4
Pittman's Field CM20 . . . **27** B1
Plain The CM16 . . . . **39** A3
Plashets CM22 . . . . **20** B2
Plaw Hatch Cl CM23 . . . . **14** A4
Plaw Hatch Cnr CM23 . . **14** C4
Playhouse Sq CM20 . . . . **32** B4
Pleasant Rd CM23 . . . . . . **11** A2
Ploughmans Cl CM23 . . . **12** B3
Ployters Rd CM18 . . . . . . **36** B4
Pollard Hatch CM19 . . . . **32** A1
Pond La
Hatfield Heath CM22 . . . . . **21** B3
Stansted Mountfitchet
CM24 . . . . **4** A3
Poole St CO10 . . . . **18** B1
Poplar Cotts CM17 . . . . . **35** A1
Portland Pl **17** CM23 . . . . **11** B1
Portland Rd CM23 . . . . . . **11** B1
Post Office Cotts CM22 . . **2** B3
Post Office Rd CM20 . . . . **26** C1
Potters Field CM17 . . . . . **34** C4
Potter St
Bishop's Stortford
CM23 . . . . **11** B1
Harlow CM17 . . . . **34** B2
POTTER STREET **34** C2
Potter Street Prim Sch
CM17 . . . . **34** C2
Poulteney Rd CM24 . . . . . **4** B4
Prentice Pl CM17 . . . . . . **34** B2
Prestwick Dr CM23 . . . . . **5** A1
Primley La CM22 . . . . **20** A2
Primrose Cl CM23 . . . . . . **12** B4
Primrose Field CM18 . . . **33** B1
Princes Cl CM16 . . . . **43** B3
Princes Ct CM23 . . . . **10** B1
Princes Gate CM23 . . . . . **10** B1
Princes Gate CM20 . . . . . **27** A3
Princess Alexandra Hospl
CM20 . . . . **26** B1
Printers Way CM20 . . . . . **22** A1
Priors **8** CM23 . . . . **11** C1
Priors Ct CM22 . . . . **19** C2
Prior's Wood Rd CM22 . . **17** A3
Priory Ave CM17 . . . . **22** C1
Priory Cl CB10 . . . . **21** B4
Priory Ct
Bishop's Stortford
CM23 . . . . **11** B1
Harlow CM18 . . . . **34** A1
Priory Dr CM24 . . . . **4** B1
Priory Wood Rdbt
CM22 . . . . **15** C4
Proctors Way CM23 . . . . **13** C2
Pryors Cl CM23 . . . . **13** C4
Pump Ho The **13** CM23 . . **11** C1
Purford Gn CM18 . . . . . . **33** C3

Purford Green Jun & Inf
Schs CM18 . . . . **33** C2
Pye Gdns CM23 . . . . **11** A2
Pyenest Rd CM19 . . . . . . **32** B2
Pynchbek CM23 . . . . **13** A1
Pynchon Paddocks
CM22 . . . . **2** C2
Pypers Hatch CM20 . . . . **33** B4
Pytt Field CM17 . . . . **34** A3

Q

Quarry Spring CM20 . . . . **33** C4
Queens Cl CM24 . . . . **4** B4
Queen's Cl CM21 . . . . **19** B4
Queens Cres CM23 . . . . . **13** A3
Queensgate Ctr CM20 . . **27** B4
Queens Rd CM16 . . . . . . **43** A3
Queensway CM5 . . . . **44** A2

R

Radburn Cl CM18 . . . . . . **37** C4
Radwinter Rd
Ashdon CB10 . . . . **34** A3
Saffron Walden CB10 . . . . **36** A1
Sewards End CB10 . . . . . . **37** B1
Rahn Rd CM16 . . . . **41** A4
Rainsford Rd CM24 . . . . . . **4** B4
Ramblers La **5** CM17 . . **28** C1
Ram Gorse CM20 . . . . . . **26** A2
Ranulf Cl CM17 . . . . **22** C2
Ravensmere CM16 . . . . . **38** C1
Rayfield CM16 . . . . **38** C2
Rayments Bglws CB10 . . **38** A3
Raynham Cl CM23 . . . . . **14** B3
Raynham Rd CM23 . . . . . **14** A4
Readings The CM18 . . . . **33** B1
Recreation Ground
CM24 . . . . **4** B2
Rectory Cl CM23 . . . . **12** C1
Rectory Field CM19 . . . . **32** A2
Rectory La CM19 . . . . **32** A2
Rectory Wood CM20 . . . . **26** B1
Redbrick Row CM22 . . . . . **2** A3
Red Cotts CM22 . . . . **20** B1
Redgates La CB10 . . . . . . **37** A3
Redgrove Ho CM16 . . . . . **38** C2
Red Lion Cres CM17 . . . . **34** B2
Red Lion Ct **4** CM23 . . . **11** C1
Red Lion La CM17 . . . . . . **34** C2
Redricks La CM21 . . . . . . **22** A2
Redvers Cl CM23 . . . . . . **11** C4
Red Willow CM19 . . . . . . **31** B3
Redwoods The CM23 . . . **10** C2
Reedings Jun Sch
CM21 . . . . **19** A3
Reedings Way CM21 . . . **19** B4
Reeves La CM19 . . . . **30** C3
Regency Cl CM23 . . . . . . **11** A1
Regency Ct CM18 . . . . . . **33** C1
Regent Rd CM16 . . . . **38** B1
Reginald Mews **4**
CM17 . . . . **28** B1

Reynard Copse CM23 . . . **11** B3
Rhodes Ave CM23 . . . . . . **13** B3
Richard Whittington Prim
Sch CM23 . . . . **13** A2
Richmond Cl CM23 . . . . . **10** B1
Riddings La CM18 . . . . . . **37** C4
Ridgeways CM17 . . . . **35** A4
Ridgewell Rd
Ashen CO10 . . . . **28** B1
Birdbrook CO9 . . . . **27** A2
Ridings The CM23 . . . . . . **12** C2
Ridley Gdns CM22 . . . . **3** B3
Risdens CM18 . . . . **32** C1
River Ct CM21 . . . . **19** B3
Riverfield La CM21 . . . . . **19** A3
Rivermill CM20 . . . . **26** B2
Rivers Hospl (private) The
CM21 . . . . **18** B1
Riverside CM23 . . . . **11** B1
Riverside Bsns Pk CM24 . **4** B2
Riverside Ct CM20 . . . . . . **22** C2
Riverside Wlk **16** CM23 . **11** B1
River Way CM20 . . . . **22** B1
RO24 CM19 . . . . **24** C2
Robert Wallace Cl
CM23 . . . . **11** B3
ROBINHOOD END **44** C3
Robin Hood Rd CM22 . . . . **3** B2
Robin Jeffrey Ct **18**
CM23 . . . . **13** B4
Robinson Cl CM23 . . . . . . **13** B3
Rochford Cl CM24 . . . . **4** B1
Rochford Rd CM23 . . . . . . **5** B1
Roden Cl CM17 . . . . **29** B4
Roding View CM5 . . . . . . **44** C1
Rodney Rd CM5 . . . . **45** C4
Roman La CM24 . . . . **7** A2
Roman Rise CM21 . . . . . . **18** C2
Roman Vale CM17 . . . . . . **22** C1
ROOK END **41** A1
Rook End La CB11 . . . . . . **41** B1
Rookery The CM24 . . . . . . **4** B4
Rookes CB10 . . . . **30** C1
Roseacres
Sawbridgeworth CM21 . . . **18** C3
Takeley CM22 . . . . **17** A3
Rosebery CM23 . . . . **14** B2
Rose Cotts CM17 . . . . **35** B4
Roseley Cotts CM20 . . . . **26** A4
Rosemary Cl **1** CM17 . . **28** B4
Rosemount CM19 . . . . . . **31** C3
Roughtallys CM16 . . . . . . **42** B1
Round Coppice Rd
Great Hallingbury
CM24 . . . . **15** C4
Stansted Mountfitchet
CM24 . . . . **7** A1
Rowan Wlk CM21 . . . . . . **19** A2
Rowney Gdns CM21 . . . . **22** C4
Rowney Wood CM21 . . . . **18** B1
Rows The **1** CM20 . . . . . **26** C1
Royal Oak Gdns **6**
CM23 . . . . **13** B4
ROYDON **24** A3

Roydonbury Ind Est
CM19. . . . .**25** A2
ROYDON HAMLET **30** B2
Roydon Lodge Chalet Est
CM19. . . . .**24** B3
Roydon Prim Sch
CM19. . . . .**24** A4
Roydon Rd CM19. . . . .**25** A3
Roydon Sta CM19 . . . .**24** A4
Rumballs Ct CM23. . . . . .**12** B2
Rundells CM18. . . . .**37** C4
Rushes Ct CM23. . . . .**13** C3
Rushes Mead CM18 . . . .**33** A2
Rushfield CM21 . . . .**19** A2
Rush La CM22. . . . . **3** B2
Rushleigh Gn CM23 . . . .**12** C2
Rushton Gr CM17 . . . . . .**35** A4
Ryecroft CM19 . . . .**32** A4
RYE HILL **37** A1
Rye Hill Rd CM18. . . . . . .**37** A2
Rye St CM23 . . . .**11** B3

S

Saddlers Cl CM23 . . . . . .**12** B2
Sadlers Mead CM18 . . . .**33** C3
SAFFRON WALDEN. . . .**31** A1
St Albans RC Prim Sch
CM20. . . . .**27** B2
St Alban's Rd CM16 . . . .**39** C2
St Andrews CE Prim Sch
CM16. . . . .**43** B3
St Andrews Cl CM16. . . .**43** C4
St Andrew's Ho CM20 . .**27** B2
St Andrew's Mdw CM18 **33** B3
St Catherines Ct CM23. .**11** A1
St Edmund's Way CM17 **28** B4
St Gregorys Ho CM16. . .**41** A4
St Helen's Ct CM16. . . . .**38** C1
St James' Ave CM5 . . . . .**45** B2
St James CE Prim Sch
CM18. . . . .**36** C4
St James Ctr CM20. . . . .**27** C4
St James Way CM23 . . . .**12** B1
St John's Ave CM17 . . . .**28** B4
St John's CE Sch CM16 **38** A1
St John's Cres CM24 . . . . **4** B3
St John's La CM24 . . . . . . **4** B3
St John's Rd
Epping CM16 . . . .**38** B1
Stansted Mountfitchet
CM24 . . . . **4** B3
St Johns Wlk CM17. . . . .**28** B4
St Joseph's RC Prim Sch
CM23. . . . .**13** A4
St Luke's RC Prim Sch
CM19. . . . .**32** B2
St Margaret's Hospl
CM16. . . . .**39** A2
St Mark's West Essex RC
Sch CM18. . . . .**33** A3
St Martin's Mews CM5. . **45** B3
St Mary's CE Foundation
Prim Sch CM24. . . . . **4** B3

St Mary's Dr CM24 . . . . . . **4** C1
St Mary's RC Sch CM23 **11** A1
St Marys View CB10 . . . .**31** A2
St Michael's CE Prim Sch
CM23. . . . .**11** B1
St Michaels Cl CM20 . . . .**27** A1
ST MICHAEL'S MEAD . . **12** B3
St Nicholas Gn **1**
CM17. . . . .**28** C1
St Nicholas Sch CM17 . .**29** B3
St Peter's Ave CM5 . . . . .**44** B2
St Valery CM22 . . . .**17** A3
Sakins Croft CM18 . . . . .**33** B1
Salisbury Cl CM23. . . . . .**13** B3
Salters CM23 . . . .**12** B2
Sanders Cl CM24. . . . . . . **4** B3
Sandle Rd CM23 . . . .**11** C1
Sandon Pl CM5 . . . .**45** B2
Sandpiper Ct **16** CM23. .**13** B4
Sandringham Ave
CM19. . . . .**25** A2
Sandringham Gdns **6**
CM23. . . . .**13** A3
Sappers Cl CM21. . . . . . .**19** B2
Sarah's Wlk CM22. . . . . .**16** C3
Sarbir Ind Pk CM17. . . . .**22** C1
Saunders Cl CM22. . . . . . **3** B2
Savoy Wood CM19 . . . . .**36** A2
SAWBRIDGEWORTH **18** B3
Sawbridgeworth Rd
Hatfield Heath CM22. . . . .**20** B4
Little Hallingbury CM22. . . .**2** A1
Sawbridgeworth Sta
CM21. . . . .**19** C3
Sayesbury Ave CM21 . . .**19** A3
Sayesbury Rd CM21 . . . .**19** A2
Sayes Gdns CM21 . . . . . .**19** B2
School Green La CM16 . **43** B3
School La CM20. . . . .**27** A2
Scimitar Pk CM19 . . . . . .**25** B3
Scott Rd CM23 . . . .**13** A4
Second Ave
Harlow CM18, CM20 . . . . .**33** B4
Stansted Mountfitchet
CM24 . . . . **7** A2
Seeleys CM17. . . . .**28** B4
Service Industry Bays
CM20. . . . .**27** B2
Seventh Ave CM24 . . . . . **7** A2
Severns Field CM16 . . . .**38** C2
SEWARDS END. **37** A1
Sewell Harris Cl CM20. .**27** B1
Seymour Mews CM21. . .**23** B3
Seymours
Harlow CM19. . . . .**31** B3
Harlow CM19. . . . .**31** C3
Shackleton Gdns CM23 **13** A4
Shaftesbury Rd CM16 . .**38** B2
Shakletons CM5 . . . .**45** B4
Shangani Rd CM23 . . . . .**13** B3
Sharpecroft CM19. . . . . .**32** B4
Shawbridge CM19. . . . . .**32** B1
Shaw The CM22 . . . .**21** B4
Shearers The CM23. . . . .**12** B2

SHEERING **20** B1
Sheering CE Prim Sch
CM22. . . . .**20** B1
Sheering Dr CM17. . . . . .**29** A4
Sheering Lower Rd
CM21. . . . .**19** C2
Sheering Mill La CM21 . .**19** B2
Sheering Rd CM17 . . . . .**29** B4
Sheldon Cl CM17. . . . . . .**35** A4
SHELLEY **44** A2
Shelley Cl CM5. . . . .**44** A2
Shelley Prim Sch CM5 . .**44** A2
Shenfield Ct CM18 . . . . .**32** B1
Shenval Ho CM20 . . . . . .**27** C4
Shenval Ind Est CM20 . .**27** C4
Shepherds Cl CM23 . . . .**12** B2
Sheppards CM19. . . . . . .**31** B3
Sherards Ho CM19 . . . . .**32** A2
Sherards Orch CM19 . . .**32** A2
Sherwood Ct **20** CM23 . .**11** B1
Sherwood Ho CM18 . . . .**33** B2
Shortcroft CM23 . . . .**14** C3
Shortlands Ave CM5. . . .**44** A2
Shortlands Pl CM23 . . . .**11** B2
Shrublands CB10. . . . . . .**31** A1
Sibneys Gn CM18. . . . . . .**37** A4
Sidings The CO10 . . . . . .**20** A3
Sidney Terr CM23 . . . . . .**13** B4
Silk Factory Row CO10 . . **2** A1
Silver Birch Ave CM16 . .**42** A1
Silver St CM24 . . . . **4** A2
Silverwood Cl EN9 . . . . .**31** A1
Simon Campion Ct
CM16. . . . .**38** C1
Simplicity La **6** CM17 . .**28** C1
Sixth Ave CM24 . . . . **7** B3
Skinners St CM23 . . . . . .**12** B2
Slacksbury Hatch
CM19. . . . .**32** A4
Slade The CB10 . . . .**25** B1
Smiths Gn CB11. . . . .**41** C2
SMITH'S GREEN. **17** B3
Smithy The CM21. . . . . . .**19** A3
Snowdrop Cl CM23 . . . . .**12** B4
Snowley Par CM23 . . . . . . **5** A1
Soper Sq **2** CM17. . . . . .**28** B1
South Block CM21. . . . . .**19** B2
Southbrook CM21. . . . . .**19** A1
Southern Lodge CM19. .**32** B1
Southern Way CM18. . . .**32** C1
Southfield CB10. . . . .**21** B4
South Gate CM20 . . . . . .**32** C4
Southmill Ct CM23 . . . . .**13** C4
Southmill Rd CM23. . . . .**13** C3
Southmill Trad Ctr
CM23. . . . .**13** C4
South Pl CM20. . . . .**27** C4
South Rd
Bishop's Stortford
CM23. . . . .**13** C3
Harlow CM20. . . . .**27** C4
Takeley CM22 . . . .**17** A4
South St Commercial Ctr
1 CM23 . . . .**13** B4

South St CM23 . . . .**13** B4
Sovereign Ct CM19 . . . . .**32** A1
Sparepenny La N CB10 .**42** C1
Sparepenny La S CB10. .**43** A1
Spencer Cl
Elsenham CM22. . . . . **3** B4
Epping CM16 . . . .**39** A2
Stansted Mountfitchet
CM24 . . . . **4** B2
Spencer Ho CM24 . . . . . .**4** A3
Spencers Croft CM18. . .**34** C2
Spinney Ct CM21 . . . .**19** A2
Spinney Jun & Inf Schs
CM20. . . . .**27** C1
Spinney The
Chipping Ongar CM5 . . . . .**45** A2
1 *Harlow* CM20. . . . .**27** C1
Stansted Mountfitchet
CM24 . . . . **4** B2
Spinning Wheel Mead
CM18. . . . .**33** C1
Spire Green Ctr CM19 . .**25** A1
Spires The CM23 . . . .**10** C1
Spriggs Ct CM16 . . . .**38** C2
Spriggs Oak CM16 . . . . .**38** C2
Springfield CM16 . . . . . .**40** C3
Springfield Cl CM5. . . . .**44** A2
Springfield Ct CM23. . . .**11** A2
Springhall Ct CM21. . . . .**19** A2
Springhall La CM21 . . . .**19** A1
Springhall Rd CM21. . . .**19** A2
Spring Hills CM20 . . . . . .**26** A1
Spring Hills Twr CM20 . .**25** C3
Spring Mdw CO10 . . . . . . **2** A1
Spring Mews CM21. . . . .**19** A2
Spruce Hill CM18 . . . . . .**37** A3
Square St **3** CM17. . . . .**28** B1
Square The CM21 . . . . . .**19** A2
Squires Cl CM23 . . . .**10** B2
Squirrels Cl **2** CM23 . . .**11** B2
Stacey Ct **9** CM23 . . . . .**13** B4
Stackfield CM20 . . . .**27** C3
Stackyard The CB10 . . . .**21** B4
Staddles CM22. . . . . **2** A3
Stadium Way CM19. . . . .**25** B3
Stafford Ho CM23 . . . . . .**13** B3
Staffords CM17 . . . .**29** A4
Stainers CM23 . . . .**12** B3
Standingford CM19. . . . .**36** A3
Stane Cl CM23 . . . .**11** B3
Stanfields Ct CM20 . . . . .**27** A1
Stanford Rivers Rd
CM5. . . . .**45** B1
Stanley Pl CM5. . . . .**45** B3
Stansted Airport Sta
CM24 . . . . **9** A4
Stansted Ctyd CM24. . . . . **9** A1
STANSTED
MOUNTFITCHET. **4** B4
Stansted Mountfitchet Sta
CM24. . . . . **4** B2

Stansted Rd
Birchanger CM23..........**5** B4
Bishop's Stortford CM23...**5** A2
Elsenham CM22..........**3** B2
Stantons CM20..........**26** A1
Staple Tye CM18..........**32** C1
Staple Tye Sh Mews
CM18.................**32** B1
Star La CM16 ....**38** C1
Starling Ct **17** CM23 ....**13** B4
START HILL **15** C3
Station App CM20......**22** C1
Station Ct CM5.........**45** B4
Station Rd
Birdbrook CO9..........**26** C1
Bishop's Stortford CM23...**11** C1
Elsenham CM22..........**3** B3
Epping CM16...........**41** A4
Harlow CM17...........**28** B4
North Weald Bassett
CM16 ....**43** A1
Sawbridgeworth CM21 ...**19** B3
Stansted Mountfitchet
CM24 ....**4** B2
Takeley CM22 ....**17** A3
Steeple View CM23 .....**11** B2
STEWARDS **37** A3
Stewards Cl CM16......**41** A2
STEWARD'S GREEN ...**41** B3
Stewards Green Rd
CM16.................**41** B2
Stewards Sch CM18 ...**36** C4
Stewarts The CM23.....**13** A4
Stile Croft CM18 ....**33** C2
Stockmen Field CM23 ..**12** B3
STOKE BY CLARE......**28** B4
Stoke Coll CO10........**28** B3
Stonards Hill CM16......**41** C4
Stondon Rd CM5.......**45** C2
Stone Cross **3** CM20 ...**26** C1
Stoneleigh CM21.......**18** C3
Stoney Comm CM24.....**4** B1
Stoney Common Rd
CM24 ....**4** A1
Stoneyfield Dr CM24 .....**4** B2
Stoney Pl CM24 ....**4** B1
Stony Wood CM18......**33** A3
Stortford Hall Ind Pk
CM23.................**14** A3
Stortford Hall Pk CM23 .**14** A4
Stortford Hall Rd 3
CM23.................**14** A4
STORTFORD PARK.....**10** B2
Stort Lodge CM23......**10** C2
Stort Mill CM20 ....**22** B2
Stort Rd CM23 ....**13** B4
Stort Valley Ind Pk
CM23.................**5** A2
Stour Cl CO10..........**20** A3
Stour Vale CO10........**26** C2
Stow The CM20 ....**27** B2

Street The
Ashen CO10............**28** C1
Sheering CM22 ....**20** A1
Stoke by C CO10 ....**28** A3
Sue Ryder Foundation
Mus* CO10 ....**18** C1
Summercroft Prim Sch
CM23.................**14** B4
SUMNERS **31** C2
Sumners Farm Cl
CM19.................**31** C1
Sunningdale CM23 .....**13** A4
Sunny Croft CM18......**33** B1
Sunnyside CM24 ....**4** B2
Sunnyside Rd CM16 ...**40** C3
Sun St CM21...........**19** B1
Sutton Acres CM22......**2** C2
Swallow Ct CM23 ......**13** C4
Swallows CM17 ....**28** B4
Swan Ct **2** CM23......**13** B4
Sweet Briar CM23......**12** A4
Sweet Mead CB10......**31** A1
Sweyns CM17 ....**34** B2
Sworders Yd **3** CM23 ..**11** B1
Sycamore Cl CM22 .....**17** A3
Sycamore Field CM19 ..**31** C3
Sycamores The CM23...**14** A2
Sylvesters CM19 ....**31** B4

T

Tailors CM23..........**12** A3
TAKELEY **17** A4
Takeley Bsns Ctr CM22..**17** A3
Takeley Pk CM22 ......**17** A2
Takeley Prim Sch
CM22.................**17** A4
Tall Trees Cvn Pk CM24 ..**6** C4
Tanys Ct CM20 ....**27** B3
Tany's Dell CM20.......**27** C3
Tany's Dell Com Prim Sch
CM20.................**27** C3
Tarlings CM20 ....**27** B3
Tatton St **6** CM17.....**28** B1
Tawneys Rd CM18......**33** B2
Taylifers CM19.........**31** C1
Taylors End Rd CM24 ....**8** A1
Tempest Mead CM16 ..**43** A1
Temple Bank CM20.....**22** B1
TEMPLE FIELDS........**27** C4
Templefields Ent Ctr
CM20.................**27** C3
Temple Mead CM19 ....**24** A3
Tendring Mews CM18 ..**33** A3
Tendring Rd CM18 .....**33** A2
Tennyson Ho CM16.....**41** A4
Tenth Ave CM24.........**7** B2
Terlings Pk CM20 ......**26** C4
Terminal Rd N CM22,
CM24.................**9** A4
Terminal Rd S CM22,
CM24.................**9** A4
Terminus St CM20......**26** C1
Terrace The CO10 .....**18** C1

Thatchers The CM23....**12** B3
Thaxted Rd CB11......**41** C2
The Maltings CM21.....**19** B2
Theydon Bower CM16 ..**41** A4
Theydon Gr CM16 .....**38** C1
Theydon Pl CM16 .....**40** C4
Theydon Rd CM16......**40** A2
Third Ave
Harlow CM18, CM19 ....**32** B3
Stansted Mountfitchet
CM24 ....**7** A2
Thomas Heskin Ct 10
CM23.................**11** C1
Thorley Hill CM23 .....**13** B3
Thorley Hill Prim Sch
CM23.................**13** B2
Thorley La
Bishop's Stortford, Thorley
Houses CM23.........**12** A3
Bishop's Stortford, Thorley
Park CM23 ....**12** C1
Bishop's Stortford, Thorley
Street CM23..........**13** B1
Thorley Neighbourhood
Ctr CM23 ....**12** C2
THORLEY PARK **12** C2
Thorley Park Rd CM23..**13** B2
THORLEY STREET **13** B1
Thornbera CM23........**13** B2
Thornbera Gdns CM23..**13** B2
Thornbera Rd CM23....**13** B2
Thornfield Rd CM23 ...**11** A2
Thorn Gr CM23.........**14** A2
Thorn Grove Prim Sch
CM23.................**14** A2
Thornhill CM16 ....**43** B2
Thornwood Rd CM16 ..**39** A3
Three Horseshoes Rd
CM19.................**32** A2
Thremhall Ave
Bishop's Stortford
CM23 ....**15** B4
Takeley CM24 ....**8** C2
Thresher Cl CM23 .....**12** B3
Thurstans CM19.......**36** B3
Tickenhall Dr CM17 ....**34** C3
Tidy's La CM16........**39** A2
Tilbury Mead CM18 ....**33** C2
Tilegate Ho CM18 .....**33** B2
Tilegate Rd CM18 .....**33** B2
Tillwicks Rd CM18.....**33** C2
TINDON END..........**38** C1
Tindon End Rd CB10...**39** C2
Tithelands CM19.......**31** C3
Toddbrook CM19.......**32** A3
Top Rd CB10.........**38** A3
Tot La CM23, CM24.......**5** C4
Tower Cl CM16........**43** C4
Tower Ct CM5.........**45** B3
Tower Rd CM16 ....**38** B1
TOWN PARK **27** A2
Tracyes Rd CM18......**34** A2
Trinity Cl CM23.........**13** B4
Trinity St CM23 ....**13** B4

Trinity Way CM23 ......**13** B4
Tripton Rd CM18 ......**33** A3
Trojan Terr CM21......**19** A3
Trotters Rd CM18 ......**33** C1
Tucker's Row **4** CM23..**13** B4
Tudor Ct CM21.........**19** A3
Tumbler Rd CM18 .....**34** A3
Tunnmeade CM20......**27** C1
Turners Cl CM5........**45** A3
Turners Cres CM23.....**12** B2
Turnors CM20.........**32** B4
Turret Ct CM5.........**45** B3
Twenty First St CM24....**8** B3
Twyford Bsns Ctr The
CM23.................**13** C2
Twyford Bury La CM22,
CM23.................**13** C2
Twyford Cl CM23 ....**13** C3
Twyford Gdns CM23 ...**13** B2
Twyford Ind Est CM23 ..**13** C1
Twyford Mews CM22 ..**13** C1
Twyford Mill CM22 ....**13** C1
Twyford Rd CM23 .....**13** C3
TYE GREEN **33** A2
Tye Green Village
CM18.................**33** B1
Tylers CB10...........**37** A1
TYLERSCROSS **31** A1
TYLER'S GREEN **43** C4
Tylers Rd CM19 ....**30** C1
Tylney Croft CM19......**32** A2
Tysea Cl CM18 ....**33** B1
Tysea Rd CM18.........**33** B1

U

Upper Gn CO10 ....**28** B4
Upper Hook CM18......**33** B2
Upper Mealines CM18 ..**33** C1
Upper Pk CM20 ....**26** A1
Upper Stonyfield CM19 .**32** A4
Upper Swaines CM16...**38** B1
Urban Rd CM23 ....**14** A3
Usterdale Rd CB10 .....**31** A1

V

Valley Ct CM23.........**13** A3
Vantorts Cl CM21.......**19** A2
Vantorts Rd CM21......**19** A2
Velizy Ave CM20........**26** C1
Vernon Ct CM23.......**13** A2
Vicarage Cl **18** CM23 ...**11** B1
Vicarage La
North Weald Bassett
CM16 ....**43** A4
North Weald Bassett, Tyler's
Green CM16..........**43** C4
Vicarage Rd CM16......**39** B2
Vicarage Wood CM20...**27** C1
Vicerons Pl CM23 ......**12** C2
Victoria Ct CM20 ......**27** A1
Villiers-Sur-Marne Ave
CM23.................**12** C2

Wagon Mead CM22. . . . . **21** B4
Wainwright St CM23. . . . **12** B3
Walden Rd
  Ashdon CB10. . . . . **33** A2
  Sewards End CB10 . . . . . . **36** C1
Walfords Cl CM17 . . . . . . **28** B3
Walnut Cotts CM21. . . . . **19** A3
Walnut Dr CM23 . . . . **12** C1
Walnut Gr CM20. . . . . **26** A1
Walnut Tree Ave CM21. . **19** A4
Walnut Tree Cres
  CM21. . . . . **19** A3
Walter Mead Cl CM5 . . . **44** B1
Ward Cres CM23 . . . . **13** A4
Ward Hatch CM20 . . . . . . **27** C3
Warish Hall Farm CM24. . **9** C1
Warren Cl CM22. . . . . **17** B3
Warren Field CM16. . . . . . **41** A3
Warwick Rd
  Bishop's Stortford
  CM23 . . . . **14** A2
  Takeley CM6 . . . . **17** C3
WATER END. **34** A2
Waterhouse Moor
  CM18. . . . . **33** B3
Water La
  Bishop's Stortford
  CM23 . . . . **11** B2
  Cavendish CO10 . . . . **18** C2
  Harlow CM19. . . . . **31** C3
  Roydon CM19 . . . . **31** A2
  Stansted Mountfitchet
  CM24 . . . . **4** B2
Water Lane Prim Sch
  CM19. . . . . **31** C2
Watermans Way CM16. . **42** C1
Waterside CM24 . . . . **4** B2
Waterside Pl CM22 . . . . . **19** C2
Watersmeet CM19 . . . . . . **36** A4
Watlington Rd CM17 . . . **28** C4
Watson's Cl CB10 . . . . . . **43** A1
Watsons Yd 🟥 CM23 . . . **11** B2
Wayletts Dr CM23 . . . . . . **14** A3

Wayre St CM17. . . . . **28** B4
Wayre The CM17 . . . . **28** B4
Waytemore Castle*
  CM23. . . . . **11** C1
Waytemore Rd CM23 . . . **13** A4
Weald Hall La CM16 . . . . **42** A3
Weaver St CM23 . . . . **12** B2
Wedgewood Cl CM16. . . **38** C1
Wedgewood Dr CM17 . . **35** A3
Wedhey CM19. . . . . **32** B4
Wellesley CM19 . . . . **31** C1
Wellington Rd CM16. . . . **42** C1
Well La
  Harlow CM19. . . . . **25** C3
  Harlow CM20. . . . . **25** C2
Wentworth Dr CM23. . . . **12** C4
Westbury Rise CM17 . . . **34** C3
West Ct CM21 . . . . **19** A3
Western Ave CM16 . . . . . **40** C3
Westfield CM18 . . . . **33** A3
Westfield Cl CM23. . . . . . **11** A2
Westfield Rd CM23 . . . . . **11** A2
West Gate
  🟥 Harlow CM20. . . . . . . **26** B1
  Harlow CM20. . . . . **32** B4
West Hayes CM22 . . . . . . **21** B4
Westley La CB10 . . . . **30** C3
West Pl CM20 . . . . **27** C3
West Rd
  Bishop's Stortford
  CM23 . . . . **13** A4
  Harlow CM20. . . . . **27** C4
  Sawbridgeworth CM21 . . **18** B3
  Stansted Mountfitchet
  CM24 . . . . **4** B2
Westside Bsns Ctr
  CM19. . . . . **25** B1
West Sq 🟥 CM20. . . . . . . **26** B1
West View CM22. . . . . **17** A4
West Wlk CM20 . . . . **32** B4
Wetherfield CM24 . . . . . . **4** A3
Wetherly Cl CM17 . . . . . . **29** B4
Wharf Pl CM23. . . . . **13** C4
Wharf Rd 🟥 CM23 . . . . . **13** B4
Wharley Hook CM18. . . . **33** C1

Wheat Croft CM23. . . . . . **13** A2
Wheatfields CM17. . . . . . **23** A2
Wheatley Cl CM21. . . . . . **18** B1
Wheelers CM16 . . . . **38** C2
Wheelers Farm Gdns
  CM16. . . . . **43** A2
Wheelwrights Cl CM23 . **12** B2
Whieldon Grange
  CM17. . . . . **35** A3
White Bear CM24 . . . . **4** B4
Whitehall Est CM19 . . . . **25** A1
Whitehall La CM23 . . . . . **11** B3
Whitehall Rd CM23 . . . . . **11** A3
Whitepost Ct CM23. . . . . **13** C3
White Post Field CM21 . **18** C2
Whitewaits CM20 . . . . . . **27** A1
Whitlands CO10 . . . . **2** A1
Whittington Way CM23 . **13** B1
William Martin CE Jun &
  Inf Schs CM18. . . . . **33** B2
Willow Cl CM23 . . . . **11** A2
Willowfield CM18 . . . . . . **32** C2
Willow Mead CM21. . . . . **19** A2
Will's Ayley La CB10 . . . . **37** B2
Wilson Cl CM23 . . . . **13** B3
Wilton Cl CM23 . . . . **14** A3
WIMBISH GREEN **38** A3
Wimborne Cl CM21. . . . . **18** C2
Winchester Cl CM23. . . . **12** C2
Windhill CM23 . . . . **11** A1
Windhill Old Rd CM23 . . **11** A1
Windhill Prim Sch
  CM23. . . . . **13** A4
Windmill Cl CM24 . . . . **4** B3
Windmill Fields CM17 . . **29** B4
Windmill Hill CB10,
  CB11 . . . . **30** A1
Windmill The CM24. . . . . . **4** A2
Windsor Gdns CM23. . . . **10** B1
Wisemans Gdns CM21 . . **18** B1
Wissants CM19. . . . . **36** B4
Woburn Ave CM23. . . . . . **10** B1
Woodberry Down
  CM16. . . . . **38** C3
Woodbine Cl CM19 . . . . . **32** B2

Woodcroft CM18 . . . . **32** C2
Woodfield Cl CM24. . . . . . **4** B2
Woodfields CM24 . . . . **4** B2
Woodfield Terr CM24 . . . . **4** B2
Woodhall Gr CM23 . . . . . **12** C4
Woodhill CM18 . . . . **33** A1
Wooding Gr CM19. . . . . . **32** A4
Wood La CM23. . . . . **6** A2
Woodland Gr CM16. . . . . **41** A3
Woodlands
  Bishop's Stortford
  CM23 . . . . **14** B4
  Epping CM16 . . . . **41** A4
Woodland Way CM5 . . . . **45** A2
Woodleys CM20 . . . . **27** C1
Wood Meads CM16. . . . . **39** A2
Woodpecker Cl CM23. . . **12** B4
Woodredon Cl CM19 . . . **24** A1
Woodside CM23. . . . . **14** C4
Woodwards CM19 . . . . . . **32** B2
Woodyard The CM16. . . . **39** B3
Wraglins The CM23. . . . . **14** A1
Wrenbrook Rd CM23 . . . **13** B4
Wrens The CM19 . . . . **32** A4
Wrights Ct CM17 . . . . **34** B2
WRIGHT'S GREEN **2** C2
Wrights Green La CM22 . **2** C2
Wych Elm CM20. . . . . **26** B1
Wychford Dr CM21 . . . . . **18** B1
Wyldwood Cl CM17. . . . . **22** C2

Y

Yeomans Cl CM23 . . . . . . **12** C4
Yewlands CM21 . . . . **19** A1
Yew Tree Pl CM23 . . . . . . **11** B2
Yorkes CM18. . . . . **33** B1
York Rd CM16. . . . . **42** C1

Z

Zambesi Rd CM23 . . . . . . **13** B3

List of numbered locations

In some busy areas of the maps it is not always possible to show the name of every place.

Where not all names will fit, some smaller places are shown by a number. If you wish to find out the name associated with a number, use this listing.

The places in this list are also listed normally in the Index.

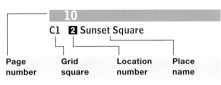

Page number	Grid square	Location number	Place name

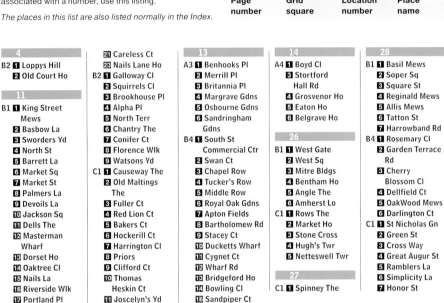

4
B2 **1** Loppys Hill
2 Old Court Ho

11
B1 **1** King Street Mews
2 Basbow La
3 Sworders Yd
4 North St
5 Barrett La
6 Market Sq
7 Market St
8 Palmers La
9 Devoils La
10 Jackson Sq
11 Dells The
12 Masterman Wharf
13 Dorset Ho
14 Oaktree Cl
15 Nails La
16 Riverside Wlk
17 Portland Pl
18 Vicarage Cl
19 Grove Pl
20 Sherwood Ct

21 Careless Ct
22 Nails Lane Ho
B2 **1** Galloway Cl
2 Squirrels Cl
3 Brookhouse Pl
4 Alpha Pl
5 North Terr
6 Chantry The
7 Conifer Ct
8 Florence Wlk
9 Watsons Yd
C1 **1** Causeway The
2 Old Maltings The
3 Fuller Ct
4 Red Lion Ct
5 Bakers Ct
6 Hockerill Ct
7 Harrington Cl
8 Priors
9 Clifford Ct
10 Thomas Heskin Ct
11 Joscelyn's Yd
12 Jubilee Cott
13 Pump Ho The

13
A3 **1** Benhooks Pl
2 Merrill Pl
3 Britannia Pl
4 Margrave Gdns
5 Osbourne Gdns
6 Sandringham Gdns
B4 **1** South St Commercial Ctr
2 Swan Ct
3 Chapel Row
4 Tucker's Row
5 Middle Row
6 Royal Oak Gdns
7 Apton Fields
8 Bartholomew Rd
9 Stacey Ct
10 Ducketts Wharf
11 Cygnet Ct
12 Wharf Rd
13 Bridgeford Ho
14 Bowling Cl
15 Sandpiper Ct
16 Starling Cl
17 Robin Jeffrey Ct

14
A4 **1** Boyd Cl
3 Stortford Hall Rd
4 Grosvenor Ho
5 Eaton Ho
6 Belgrave Ho

26
B1 **1** West Gate
2 West Sq
3 Mitre Bldgs
4 Bentham Ho
5 Angle The
6 Amherst Lo
C1 **1** Rows The
2 Market Ho
3 Stone Cross
4 Hugh's Twr
5 Netteswell Twr

27
C1 **1** Spinney The

28
B1 **1** Basil Mews
2 Soper Sq
3 Square St
4 Reginald Mews
5 Allis Mews
6 Tatton St
7 Harrowband Rd
B4 **1** Rosemary Cl
2 Garden Terrace Rd
3 Cherry Blossom Cl
4 Dellfield Ct
5 OakWood Mews
6 Darlington Ct
C1 **1** St Nicholas Gn
2 Green St
3 Cross Way
4 Great Augur St
5 Ramblers La
6 Simplicity La
7 Honor St